UNSILENCED

How to Voice the Gospel

James Boccardo

CROSS

BOOKS

CrossBooks™
A Division of LifeWay
1663 Liberty Drive
Bloomington, IN 47403
www.crossbooks.com
Phone: 1-866-879-0502

First published by CrossBooks 05/14/10

ISBN: 978-1-6150-7174-6 (sc)

Printed in the United States of America
Bloomington, Indiana

This book is printed on acid-free paper.

A special thanks to my parents, my sister, Frank Shimkus, Ben Brooks, the Clark Family, and the staff at Southern Evangelical Seminary. Most importantly, thank you Jesus for dying for my sins and rising from the dead.

Contents

CHAPTER ONE

WHERE WERE YOU?

Where Were You?

It's party time on New Year's Eve. In my city, there are thirty thousand people walking around in a two-block area. There are also six hundred churches here, but there are no Jesus followers in sight. It's easy to spot us if we're out sharing our faith.

It's odd because we claim to know the truth. We claim to know the Son of God, Jesus the God-man. We say that faith in this Jesus is the only way to have your sin record erased. Jesus is the only One who can provide someone with eternal life. Faith in Him and His work is the only way to the Father.

If this is true, then how could Christians look on silently at all of these people? It almost seems insane. Shouldn't we be out sharing the gospel with anyone that will listen? Of course we should. But on a surface level, it seems that we don't really care. Oh sure, we care about going to Christian schools. We care about not getting drunk. But do we *really* care about the lost people right in front of us?

Maybe you're just not brave enough to venture out and talk to strangers. If you're not, have you tried to talk to the people in your neighborhood? What about people in your school? Either way, if you want to start, this book will show you how. Hopefully, the instructions and stories will encourage and show you that it isn't that hard. You can get the job done.

I Was One of Them

Thinking about this New Year's Eve situation reminds me of how I came to put my faith in Jesus.

I didn't have any certain religious tradition growing up. My family went to a church for a while when I was young, but throughout high school I wasn't really involved in any of that. I was just the average teenager that wanted to be in the NBA or be famous. I ended up going to UNC Chapel Hill and everything seemed great.

There were plenty of Christian groups on campus with hundreds of members. I was friends with some of the people who were in them, even though I wasn't a believer yet. The odd thing was that there was not a *single time* that one of them ever shared their faith with me. There wasn't a Christian who ever engaged me in a conversation about the gospel or eternal things—and they knew I wasn't one of them.

It's just like the New Year's Eve situation that we've been talking about.

There were people who tried to be friendly with me. There was one person who invited me to some of their events, and I appreciated that. But couldn't someone have taken me to lunch and asked if I wanted to hear about their Jesus? If I didn't want to hear it, I would have just said no. I didn't think that these hundreds of people knew I was in danger of dying and being judged for all my sin, and I didn't know that I could have eternal life. Not a word was ever said to me about any of that.

Everything changed for me at the end of college when I had a friend who died in a car accident. He just fell asleep at the wheel. For whatever reason, over the next year or so, it had me thinking about life after death and I actually got curious about the Bible. I read and read for a few weeks and realized something: I needed to confess my sin to God and put my faith in His Son. It is weird to think back on because there wasn't anyone discussing this with me. No one gave me anything to read about the gospel or took me out to eat to talk. It was just God at work.

I've noticed something different about people in the New Testament: they weren't silent about their faith. I think if Paul or Peter were around, I wouldn't have slipped under the radar for so long. These guys didn't just invite their friends to Christian events or to their church; they invited people to the cross. Paul explained the gospel to people and told them how and why they could have their sins forgiven. He engaged them. He talked with them. He felt responsible for the information he had about Jesus the Messiah. In Acts 26:3, he even *begged* King Agrippa to listen to him. Have you ever cared about someone so much that you begged them to listen to you about your Savior? Paul did.

So, if I got saved through reading the New Testament by myself, can you imagine what would happen to the world around us if we actually shared the gospel like the people did in the first century? Can you imagine if we took the risk and talked with our friends, much less strangers? Think of all those people in your dorm, your office, or at that festival in your town who might be willing to talk. You might be friends with an old version of myself and not even know it.

What Christians Are Known For

I think there's a reason that we are slow to share what we believe. It's because at some point in the history of the world, something changed. Christians began to be perceived as people who belong to a "religion" where the point is just better morals. And we played along. Christians are people who are *really* good while everyone else isn't. We *don't* drink or smoke. We *don't* have sex before we're married. We try to regulate society's morals. Don't … don't … don't. There sure are a lot of things we don't do.

I think outsiders get confused about our faith because, if we're really honest with ourselves, there are plenty of groups of people who *don't* do things. It's no wonder that people think that all the world's religions are the same. Jesus, Buddha, Muhammad, and whoever else you can name. They all basically teach "the same things." Mormons don't drink caffeine or watch R-rated movies. Jehovah's Witnesses don't have premarital sex or drink too much alcohol. Many Muslims disagree with abortion.

This is why we need to understand the uniqueness of our message and then we need to go share it. Everyone has sinned, and Jesus is the only One who offers forgiveness and eternal life. As soon as we forget that, we've lost what we're supposed to share with the world. So before you think that God is calling you to *only* be a housewife or a businessman, think again. You might hear a voice in your head that says that, but the Scriptures don't. The Bible tells us to do one thing that no one else in the world can do: make disciples through the power of the gospel. The gospel is what someone should have talked with me about in college and what believers should have been sharing with thousands of people on New Year's Eve. It's what we should be known for.

CHAPTER TWO

WHAT IS THE GOSPEL ANYWAY?

What Is the
Gospel Anyway?

What is this unique message that we have in the gospel? We need to understand it before we talk about how to share it. This often gets overlooked because it is assumed that everyone understands it already. I actually had someone come up to me once after I spoke at a conference and ask me, "What in the world do people mean when they say I should share the gospel? Is that the same as telling someone about Jesus?" You may want an answer to that same question too. It's okay, just keep reading.

As most know, the word "gospel" means good news. Good news is great, but good news about what? It's good news when it's sunny outside. It's also good news when the doctor tells someone that they don't have cancer, but what we're talking about here is a specific *kind* of good news, and that's what we need to share with people.

First Things First

The first thing to understand is sin. The easiest definition comes from 1 John 3:4, where John sums up it up in one word: lawlessness. First Kings 8:46 also tells us that there is no one who does not sin. That covers the basics. Sin is breaking God's law, and we've all done it. Easy enough.

God's law was given in the Old Testament. The Ten Commandments made up part of the law, and nine of the ten carry over to the New Testament (the Sabbath was left out). Here are the other nine:

1. Do not have any other gods before me.
2. Do not make or worship an idol. Including yourself.
3. Do not use God's name in vain. That means don't use it like a curse word.
4. Honor your mother and father.
5. Do not murder.
6. Do not commit adultery.
7. Do not steal.
8. Do not lie.
9. Do not covet.

These aren't rules to make you holy; they're to show you that you're not. Breaking these basic moral laws offends the God who hung the stars you see in the Hubble telescope, and it's not like we've only broken them once or twice. We've broken them thousands of times. To make the situation even worse, if God is *only* fair with us, we cannot be forgiven. God wouldn't be fair if He let the guilty into His kingdom.

In Deuteronomy 27:26, Moses tells us how severely God views our sin:

> *Cursed be anyone who does not confirm the words of this law by doing them.*

Being cursed by God doesn't sound good to me. It means you're in trouble, and it's not with the local police. It's much worse than that. So, if God just gives us what we all deserve, we would all go to hell. This is very important to understand. Anyone who dies with a guilty sin record doesn't get into the kingdom of heaven, and they would have to pay for their own sins in hell forever.

Is that it?

We would all be in trouble if that were the end of the story. Thankfully, God didn't leave us hopeless, and He planned the gospel before the world began. This is the specific kind of good news that we need to understand.

Here's what the New Testament says about it:

> In Acts 5:31, Peter says the following about Jesus:
>
> > *God then exalted him at his right hand as Leader and Savior, to give repentance to Israel and **forgiveness of sins**.*

> In Acts 10:43, Peter tells a crowd some good news about Jesus:
>
> > *All the prophets bear witness that everyone who believes in him **receives forgiveness of sins** through his name.*

> In Acts 26:18, Jesus told Paul that he is sending him to the Gentiles to:
>
> > *… open their eyes … so that they may **receive forgiveness of sins** and a place among those who are sanctified by faith in me.*

That is the good news. It's forgiveness of sins in Jesus's name. That's what we have to offer the world, and that's what we should be sharing. O*nly* Jesus's followers can share this, and it's the exact opposite of what people think of as "religion." It is uniquely good news.

How does that work?

Wait a minute. First we learned that we have sinned. Then we learned that the gospel is the unique and powerful message that all of our sins can be forgiven. How does that work? It seems like a big jump.

Everyone seems to forget that in order for God to offer anyone a clean sin record and allow the person into heaven, His anger at the individual's sin has to be placed somewhere else. After all, if I never answer for my sin, who did?

Substitution

The only reason that God can forgive anyone's sin is if someone else takes the punishment. Israel learned this well in the Old Testament when they killed animals. They would symbolically transfer the guilt of their sin onto a lamb and then kill it, but this was just a preview.

Now enter Jesus. When Jesus lived a sinless life and then hung on the cross and died, He acted as a substitute for us. Instead of God punishing the believer in Jesus after he dies, God punished His Son on the cross. Jesus became a curse, became sin, and was crushed by His Father.[1] Now we have an amazing situation:

God is not overlooking sin.

It was Jesus who took the supernatural punishment that we deserve for our sin. Just look at Him, bloody and

---

1 See Isaiah 53:6, 53:10–11; Galatians 3:13; 1 John 4:10; Romans 3:25.

bruised, hanging on that tree. And since He was punished as a substitute, God is being completely fair when he washes someone else's sin from the record books.

In most belief systems, *you* do something to turn away the anger of "the gods" for breaking their laws. In the gospel, *Jesus* did something. He did the work to turn away God's anger from you. So, when someone repents of their sin and believes in Jesus, God completely forgives that person, and the punishment that was coming their way after death is extinguished. Wouldn't you call that good news?

Now, there are some specific side effects when someone believes in this, so the gospel gets even better.

I'm "saved" and "born again"

These are phrases that people use to describe what happens to someone when they believe in Jesus, and they are important to understand. Let's make sure we know what they mean.

Saved

Paul uses this term in Romans 10. If you confess with your mouth that Jesus is Lord and that God raised Him from the dead, you will be *saved*. Saved from what? From where? When will you "be saved"?

People have told me that God needs to "save you from yourself" or "save you from the devil." I want to yell at their pastor because that's not what this means. In the New Testament, this means that you are saved from the *eternal consequences of your sin and its power over you.*

If you are saved, you're saved from hell and you have eternal life. You're saved from any judgment that would be coming your way after death. You're also saved from the overwhelming and blinding power of your sin. Now you can fight.

There was a time in college when my sister was in a conversation about these things with someone her age. The girl ended up telling my sister that there was no need to talk to her. She said that she was already "saved." My sister asked her, "From what?" and the girl said she had no idea! As you can tell, these things are important to understand.

Born Again

Jesus uses this term in John 3, and Peter uses it in one of his letters. What does it mean?

In the Old Testament, the prophets wrote about a time in the future when God would give His people a new heart.[2] In the Bible, the heart is the engine of your conscience, or the part of you that drives your moral decisions. So, being "born again" is when God supernaturally changes your heart and gives you a new one. This is also called regeneration.

I recently saw this happen to someone I know who came to faith in Jesus. One of the *first* things she told me was that she felt so different about her sin. She realized it was wrong and wanted to turn away from it. She went on to tell me about other sin in her life and how she wanted to get rid of it all. This came from a new heart that was given to her by God.

When this happens to someone, you will notice a new creature, a new creation. The old person is gone and the new one is being renewed every day, becoming more and more like Jesus.[3]

---

2 Deuteronomy 10, 30, Jeremiah 31, Ezekiel 36.
3 See Titus 3:5, 2 Corinthians 5:17, John 5:24.

Justified and Changed

Hopefully, this is all clear now. At the moment in time when someone repents of their sin and puts their faith in Jesus, they are *justified*. That means that all of their sins are completely forgiven and they are made right with God. They are *saved*. At the same time, the person is *born again* because their heart is changed by God. Because of their new heart, they will desire to turn away from sin and will see some changes in their life over time.

It's important to remember that being made right with God has nothing to do with someone doing good things. I have met so many people who think that being associated with Jesus (whatever they think that means) and doing good things add up to eternal life. Well, how much time did the criminal on the cross have to get down and do good works to make up for his sin? None! It was the criminal's *faith* in the One hanging next to him that saved him. Don't get that confused.

CHAPTER THREE

BACK TO THE FUTURE

Back to the Future

Now that we understand the basics of the gospel, we should take a quick moment to look at what the first followers of Jesus did. How did they live in light of the message they were entrusted with? If you watch closely, you'll notice that it was normal for all of them to talk about their Savior with the world around them.

It doesn't matter what First Baptist of Big City does. It doesn't matter what the Relevant Church does or what other Christians in our culture do. Don't get me wrong, it's great to have modern churches. It's great to have big churches as well. But what did the people do who actually knew Jesus personally? I want to imitate them and transport their lifestyle into mine.

I say all that because it seems like the biggest issue with Christians today is that we observe the people and events in the New Testament, but we rarely imitate the people we read about. We watch them from a distance. Let's see if you can see my point here.

Acts 4: The First Christians

In Acts 4, we see a very interesting snapshot of what the first Christians were like. Peter and John were thrown in jail in the beginning of the chapter. They were then released from prison, and they went to their friends to tell them what happened. They began to pray, and verse 24 tells us a lot:

> *And when **they** heard it, they lifted their*
> *voices **together** to God and said ...*

Who is the "they" that is praying? It was Peter, John, and *everyone else who was there*. All the Christians prayed. What did they pray? Just look at verse 29:

> *And now, Lord, look upon their threats and grant to your servants to continue to speak your word with all boldness.*

Well, there it is: each of the believers in Jesus prayed for boldness. Two verses later, they got what they asked for. There were no qualifiers here. No one had a certain gift to pray and be bold. No one "felt called" to share the gospel. They just did it. Later, in Acts 5:41, we even see Christians rejoicing because they were counted worthy to suffer for Jesus.

For believers twenty centuries later, nothing has changed. We should live the same way and be just as excited, bold, and loving as they were back then. Would anyone dare stand in front of Jesus and say otherwise?

Acts 17–18: Follow Paul Around

Well, that's just one example, right? Nope. There's more insight that the book of Acts gives us. We get it from a glimpse into Paul's life in Acts 17 and 18, and since he told us to be imitators of him, we need to see exactly what he was doing.[4]

In verse 16, Paul goes to Athens to wait for some friends. He isn't on a mission trip and he wasn't going to plant a

---

4 Paul says this at two places in his first letter to the Corinthians. He writes that in 4:16 and 11:1.

church. Now, while he was waiting, he saw all the idols there. He went to the synagogues and the marketplace, and he reasoned with the people there *every day* about the Messiah.

Stop and think for a second.

Here is a man who went from waiting for his friends in a city to sharing the gospel with the people there because of a simple observation he made: the city was full of idols. And because Paul wanted to spread the gospel like a disease, he tried to reach people every day.

It's Easy to See

After looking at how the first Christians lived and what Paul's daily life looked like, we see that we have no excuses for not sharing our faith. We will have no alibis on Judgment Day. Yes, if you have repented of your sins and put your faith in Jesus, you were saved by faith alone. Your sins were washed away and paid for on the cross. But, as Paul mentions in Romans 14:12, everyone will have to give an account of himself to God on that great day. It won't be for your sin, but it certainly will be for what you did for Jesus after you got saved.

It might be exciting to read what Paul did, but for you, it's not enough. You still have some reservations or excuses before you start sharing the gospel. That's fine. We'll handle those next.

CHAPTER FOUR

THE FAMOUS EXCUSE LIST

The Famous Excuse List

People don't share their faith because of the Excuse List. The problem is that I don't think we'll be using it when we stand in front of The King, which is why these excuses need to be addressed and then thrown in the trash can. We can move on and learn how to share our faith after that.

I don't mean to make you feel guilty, but excuses such as, "I could never talk to a stranger about my faith," or "I just don't have that gift" aren't good enough. If you said something like that and you were at the NASCAR race in Charlotte a few years ago, you might be embarrassed. There were teenage girls who would go up to grown men on their motorcycles and talk to them about the gospel. If teenagers can share their faith with people, wouldn't you agree that everyone else can?

If you've never shared your faith in Jesus with anyone, you should be excited. Today is a new day and your walk with the Lord can change right now. Hopefully, your mind will be changed in the next few minutes and you will be brave enough to leave all the excuses behind. The Excuse List is not in any certain order because it doesn't matter: we should all get rid of every last one.

Excuse #1: Church Services Are the Best Way to Reach People

When we think about sharing our faith, many people think if they just invite someone to church, that's good enough. Sometimes it is and sometimes it isn't. Give me a chance to explain.

Inviting people to church (instead of just sharing the gospel with them yourself) doesn't always make sense. I've heard about churches going from one hundred people to five thousand, and everyone makes a big deal out of it. Bring your friends and they'll all get saved! Look what God is doing! Sure, God might be doing something there, but everyone forgets that the church is in a city of a million or more people. I had to take a lot of math classes in college, so I'll spare you the need to get out the calculator. Ten thousand people out of a million make up *1 percent* of the population.

There was actually an estimate a few years ago of churches in a Southern state here in the United States. The estimate went something like this: if all the current church buildings were filled to capacity, they would house less than 10 percent of the population there.

Now, is it great that there are churches full of thousands of people? Yes. But do the math. If we really want to reach everyone we can for Jesus…

They won't all fit in our buildings!

That means they can't all meet Jesus by coming to a church service. We just might have to share the gospel at other places and times.

The Traveler

The Traveler is another thing people forget about with church service evangelism. He is the guy who comes to your city for a business meeting or to visit a relative. He might be from Saudi Arabia and is just making a weeklong trip to the United States. He's not going to go to a church because he's Muslim or only in town for the day.

One example of this that I came across was when I met a few guys in a band that was touring. They were standing in front of a hotel. One was covered in tattoos and smoking. I know most Christians would overlook someone like this, so I didn't want to. I asked him about the ink on his arms, and he was happy to talk. He told me he was in a punk band just traveling through town. How would I get him to my church on Sunday? He wouldn't be here.

We were having a friendly conversation, so I just asked what he thought about life after death. Both of the guys said that they thought religion was stupid. I quickly agreed. They didn't mean the gospel; they meant self-righteous-judge-everyone-except-yourself religion. They said they knew there had to be a god but no one knew who he was, and then one of them threw in the conversation that he thinks about this kind of stuff all the time. I explained the gospel to them both, and they told me that they were glad that I had talked with them. How else would either of these guys have heard any of that if I had tried to just invite them to church?

Airports are another great place to find The Traveler, so I try to take advantage of it when I can. I had a lot of room in my carry-on bag one time before I left for a flight, so I filled the pockets up with free books when I packed my clothes. I went through the whole airport, handing out books about the gospel and talking to flight attendants who were waiting to catch the next plane and people working in the stores. I got on the plane with nothing left in those carry-on bag pockets; mission accomplished. Those people were coming and going from all different parts of the world, and I didn't want to waste those two hours of my life.

Now for the big question: why don't the thousands of people who go to churches just share their faith in Jesus with everyone they know? Maybe even people they don't know. If we have a ten thousand-member church in a city of a million, it should just make us realize that we have a lot of work left to do. We should want to win them all, and that isn't going to happen if we only share the gospel inside a building. This leads us to another point.

Excuse #2: You Don't Believe the Unheard Go to Hell

> *... And how are they to believe in him of whom they have never heard? And how are they to hear without someone preaching* [5]
>
> *-Paul the apostle -AD 55*

(Warning: you might think this section is controversial. Please read it entirely before you get mad. The conclusion at the end is the most important.)

Unfortunately, there's a certain type of person I've come across numerous times after speaking somewhere. This kind of person scares me the most, and I think it's part of the reason Christians are apathetic at times. This type of person thinks that people who don't hear about Jesus still go to heaven. Maybe it's not that extreme. It's dressed up in a suit and tie: God will give them a "second chance." Don't hear about Jesus? It's okay. God will overlook all that somehow.

This topic came up once when I was talking to a friend of mine. He said that he started going to a big church in our area, so that piqued my interest in trying to talk to him more. I've learned the hard lesson that many people wander into big churches and they never actually get saved, so I figured I should talk with him. People hear great buzzwords like "grace" or hear a sermon about marriage, but never understand the severity of meeting God outside of His Son. Since everyone in the world likes Starbucks, I set up a time when we could sit down and talk about "religion." (It's hard for me to even type that last word. Aren't you glad Jesus isn't some boring religion?)

---

5 Romans 10:14

As we began to talk, he told me about a sermon the pastor recently gave and how he mentioned the infamous "people who don't hear about Jesus." He told me the pastor told everyone that if someone doesn't hear about Jesus, God will "do the right thing." There's the suit and tie again. Go ahead, cover it up. Apparently it got elaborated on. "God is love and He is fair with people," the pastor said. In the end, he explained that the unheard get some kind of opt-out clause. Their sin gets automatically forgiven and God just lets them into heaven. While that sounds great at first (and I wish it were true), the hard thing to swallow is that it's not what the Bible says.

The consequence of saying what this pastor said is that it leads people to an I'm-so-glad-Jesus-has-forgiven-my-sin attitude, but they don't think *every other human being on the planet* needs the same thing. It'll be fine! Everyone relax.

Don't relax too quickly. Let's be careful and take a look at Scripture. Daniel 12:2 says the following:

> *And many of those who sleep in the dust of the earth shall awake, some to everlasting life, and some to shame and everlasting contempt.*

Daniel clearly says that everyone ends up in one of two places. Jesus actually echoes this and says the same kind of thing in Matthew 25:46:

> *And these will go away into eternal punishment, but the righteous into eternal life.*

Jesus and Daniel are both making a distinction here between two kinds of people: some people will go away into eternal punishment, but the righteous (the sin-forgiven Jesus followers) will go into eternal life. There is no in-between place and no one gets a do-over. As awful and scary as it is, it's true. To make this clearer, take a look at Romans 1:20 and Acts 17:26:

> *For his invisible attributes, namely, his eternal power and divine nature, have been clearly perceived, ever since the creation of the world, in the things that have been made. So they are without excuse.*

> *And he made from one man every nation of mankind to live on all the face of the earth, having determined allotted periods and the boundaries of their dwelling place, that they should seek God, in the hope that they might feel their way toward him and find him.*

> *Yet he is actually not far from each one of us.*

There it is. Man is without excuse because of the creation that he can clearly see. We can all see it, and it screams out that there must be a God. God also put people where they are in their nations so that they would seek Him and find Him. If someone does not do that, then God still holds them accountable for their sin. If God is *fair* and does the *right thing*, like the pastor at this church said, God would actually send everyone to hell. It's almost as if people get this one completely backwards.

Now, if they do seek Him and look for Him, God can certainly get them the gospel. There are countless stories of this happening. A group of remote people looked at creation and knew within their conscience that there was a God and they cried out to Him. God heard their prayers and sent someone there to give them the rest of the message: to be right with Him, you need to repent of your sins and believe in His Son.

The Ultimate Conclusion: Silence

If we really think that people who don't hear the gospel will be all right in the end, it will bring us to one logical conclusion:

We shouldn't tell them anything about Jesus.

We should all hide our Bibles and keep our mouths shut. That way everyone will get a second chance when they die. Now, you and I both know that that makes no sense, so we have to get out and share our faith in the One who rose from the dead. You might be the only person someone ever hears it from.

Excuse #3: Share Your Faith, but Be Friends First

We have all heard people say things like, "Before you share you faith with someone, you need to be friends first." Well of course you should share your faith with your friends; you just shouldn't exclude the rest of the world while you do it. The new diagram for your daily life should look like this:

A lady came up to me and thanked me once after I had finished going through how to share the gospel at a conference. She told me that she was glad someone just got up and said it's okay to talk about her faith to whomever she wanted. She said that she thought she was the only weird one there. It had been so tattooed in her mind that she needed to make friends with someone and wait for a year before she mentioned eternal things, but it's not true. You can talk to whomever you want about your faith in Jesus, and you don't even have to know them before you do it.

Now I know what you're thinking. The voice in your head says, "There's no way anyone would want to hear this," "No one wants to talk about this," or "I'll only get rejected." The list goes on and on. The scary thing is that I've found all of those things to be completely untrue, especially when it comes to strangers.

Let me introduce you to Mosab Hassan Yousef. You may have never heard of him, but his story will change your view on sharing your faith with strangers. His father was the founder of Hamas, a radical Muslim group in the Middle East. Mosab grew up in the West Bank and was raised a Muslim. He was even a leader of the Islamic Youth Movement and was in line to take over for his father.

Then he visited Jerusalem one day.

There was a young tourist who apparently walked right up to him and talked with him about Jesus. The tourist even gave him a Bible. Mosab took the Bible and began secretly comparing it to the Quran. As time went on, he realized that he was changing his mind about his beliefs. He was now going to follow Jesus. Apparently, Al-Qaeda caught wind of this and even issued a statement directed toward Hamas. They were disappointed that he was allowed to "convert" to another religion. Just dwell on that. *Al-Qaeda* heard that Mosab was now a Christian! Can you imagine living under that pressure? He left his homeland and fled to the United States, where he is now living with people from his new church home in California. In a documentary about him, a reporter asked him how he was coping with all of this. His response? "It's a low price to pay for Jesus … it is like nothing."[6]

All of this happened in this young man's life because a brave tourist gave him a Bible and shared the gospel with him. Do you honestly still think that we should only share our faith with our friends?

Just Like the Apostles

The first century Christians acted just like the tourist in Jerusalem did when he came across Mosab Yousef. They didn't rely on their friend-making abilities to spread their message, just look at the book of Acts. We've gone over some of this before, but here are some quick observations:

Acts 13:13–15   Paul preaches to Jews he doesn't know about Jesus being Messiah.

Acts 17:16–21   Paul is waiting for his friend in Athens. He obviously hasn't been here recently because he notices the city is full of idols. He shares the gospel *every day* with the people there. Paul is eventually invited to preach at the Areopagus.

Acts 18:4–5   Paul is in Corinth and was "occupied with the word." He talked with people in the synagogue *every Sabbath*.

---

6 *Escape from Hamas* documentary from Fox News.

Now, how in the world could Paul have been friends with all these people first? He was traveling all around the Mediterranean!

A few years ago, I was actually traveling to some of the places where Paul lived in Israel. We were getting some food in a hole-in-the-wall café in the northern part of the country. There was a Jewish guy my age working behind the counter, so I asked him how long he had worked there. He said he actually just got out of working in the Israeli army near Gaza. It's a dangerous place, so the conversation was easy.

"Wow, did you see anyone die?" I asked him.

"Almost, it was scary. I actually prayed a lot."

I jumped right in, "Yeah, I bet. That would scare me too. Since you were nervous about dying, what do you think happens to someone after that?" We talked for a few minutes as I directed the conversation toward Jesus and what he did on the cross for sin. He listened the whole time and had no problem talking about these things with me, even though we had just met.

Excuse #4: Most People are "Led to Jesus" Through a Close Friend

Even with the examples that were just given, the statistics say that most people are actually led to Jesus by a close friend. It's somewhere above 80 percent. That means it's obviously the best way to spread the gospel: just talk with your close friends, right?

Stop and think for a minute. If the only people we talk to about Jesus are *close friends,* then of course that would be the way most people get saved. Why? (Insert drum roll.) That's the only way they hear about Him! It's like saying most cars today are blue and then you go to the car dealership and find out that blue cars are the only ones being sold. It's conveniently self-fulfilling.

One of the roots of this problem comes from not believing the songs we sing. My favorite is "Mighty to Save." It doesn't seem like He's so mighty if we have to be best friends with people before we talk about Him. That makes it sound like He is depending on us for Him to be able to do His work. Isn't that idolatry? He needs us and our friendship-making abilities? I don't think so.

One example where I've seen strangers get saved happened on the Fourth of July a few years ago. There was a big festival in my city, and I knew it would be full of people. I saw two middle-aged women who had a younger child with them there. They all looked bored, so I figured I would try to help get rid of their boredom. I walked up to them and started talking about some things (we'll go through later), and believe it or not, after a while, *both* of the women said, "We want to put our faith in Jesus right now." They asked Jesus to forgive them of their sin right in front of me. They didn't ask me what to say or how to pray, they just did it! Now I was *not* close friends with these two middle-aged women from Africa. As horrible as it sounds, I don't even remember their names. I would have never seen them again and this was really my only chance to talk to them about these things. I don't think I should have waited to become best friends with them first.

Excuse #5: Everyone in My Area Has Heard This Already

I can promise you one thing: no matter how many churches are in your area, not everyone there has heard the gospel. They may have heard about Jesus, but they don't know what to do with Him.

One time, I met a group of kids outside an NBA game. They all went to a local church. After talking for a few minutes, I asked them, "So what does someone have to do to be right with God?" They said, "Be a good example." I'm not kidding. A good example? Wow. If being a good example gets you into heaven, then I hope I'm ready for some warm weather.

Don't assume anything about what other people around you know about Jesus. I honestly just assume that everyone in my city has never really had the gospel explained to them.

I was downtown one night in October with this exact thing in mind. There was an old white man standing on a sidewalk waiting to go somewhere to escape the frigid air. I just asked him casually, "Hey, can I ask you a quick question? Have you ever thought about what's on the other side after you die?"

Silence.

"Well, not really. I don't really know. No one has ever talked to me about it," and he just kind of half-smiled. I got a chance to talk with him for a few minutes before he had to leave. After he left, my friend who was with me just looked at me with the oh-my-goodness-not-another-one look. Another person who has never even had these things explained to him, and this man was old. Don't forget that there are six hundred churches in the city I live in, so you would think he would have heard by now.

Another time, I was in Chicago, speaking at a conference on how to share your faith in Jesus. After the conference, we went into a large Catholic church to see the paintings on the ceiling. I had another agenda, and I started talking to the doorman. I asked him how long he had worked there and talked with him for a few minutes. Eventually I asked him, "Hey, since you've been coming to church here for so long, what do you remember them teaching you about the afterlife?" He told me that he didn't really know or remember. I handed him something I usually give to people about the gospel with my contact information on it.

I looked him right in the eyes and gently told him, "Listen, I don't mean to be too direct, but did you know that Jesus died and rose from the dead so that all your sins could be completely forgiven?" He got really quiet and looked at the card I gave him, and then he looked back at me. He looked at the card and at me a second time. Then he said, "Oh ... um, wow, thank you for sharing that with me." He really said, "Wow." The girl who was driving us around after the conference almost laughed out loud because she was so excited. She told me later that she could tell he had never heard that before in his life. His face looked like he had just seen a ghost. Stories like these are the reason why you shouldn't assume anything about how much anyone has heard.

What Should We Do?

Once I started to notice the people who were already in front of me, I started to talk to them. I didn't just walk by everyone anymore. There was a security guard in my building. I just stopped and talked to him one day, and he was happy to talk and take anything I was giving out. He saw me months later and told me he remembered our conversation. He even thanked me for caring about him. I talked to the guy at a sandwich store. He was happy to listen. We actually sat down one time after work, and he wanted to hear more. All these people were just *on the way to my car* on the way home. I wasn't on the once-a-year American mission trip.

After hundreds of these conversations, I started to think about all the other people who were around me every day. Naturally, I figured that God was sending me places to share the gospel there. As simple as this is, here's an updated map:

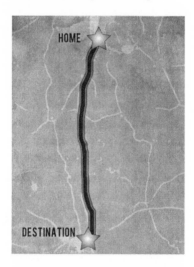

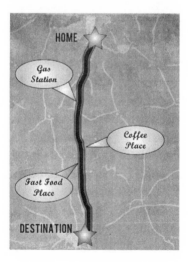

I would stop at gas stations that were off the exits of the highway. When I bought a Gatorade or filled my car up with gas, I would go in and talk to the people working there. One time, I was actually in one of these gas stations where an older woman with a Croatian accent was working. As I started talking to her, she told me this conversation meant a lot to her. She even told me, "This is very important. I have never heard any of this before."

You might think that I don't understand. You might live in Texas where there are thousands of churches. The church count in Minneapolis is one thousand. But as you can see from these stories, it doesn't matter. There are still thousands of people to reach, no matter where you are.

Excuse #6: Fear of All Kinds

Fear. It comes in different flavors.

You would think that people who are shy wouldn't be good at sharing their faith with strangers. That's only for the outgoing ones among us. It was odd, because I've never been shy, but it was hard for me to start sharing my faith as well. There must be something else going on here, and I think I know what it is: having a certain kind of personality doesn't mean you will be bold. You can be Mr. Outgoing all day long and still be a chicken when it comes to the gospel, because being *outgoing* and being *fearless for Jesus* do not necessarily go together.

The dirty little secret is that we're all a bunch of chickens, regardless of our personality type. Let's be honest. You might be scared because you don't know what to say, or you might just be scared to talk to strangers. It's time to get over it.

Fear Number One: No Words to Say

I actually had a woman walk up to me after I spoke at a church once. She said, "I've always wanted to share my faith with people, but I've never known what to say." It was amazing to hear that. She wasn't lazy; she just didn't have a clue how to start. I always wonder how many believers feel the same way.

I think this is the situation with many people in their walk with Jesus. Unfortunately, we let new believers get nice and comfortable. After a while, they just think that's the way it is. We almost train them to be silent. They don't see any brave examples and we end up producing after our own kind. I actually heard a pastor say that the best way to share your faith in Jesus is "with your lifestyle." This was in front of the two thousand people sitting there listening. Sigh.

But some people are brave and would love to share the gospel with everyone they set their eyes on. You might be one of them, but you just don't know what to say. The rest of this book will help you with that, so if this is your big fear, you'll hopefully be a recovering-from-fear Jesus follower in a short while. Just keep reading.

Fear Number Two: I'm Just Scared of People

People are also frightened to talk about their faith because they've been fed the idea that everyone is hostile toward Christians, and they'll always get rejected. That would scare anyone. If I told you a hungry tiger was waiting around the corner, then you're most likely not heading in that direction. Now, it isn't true that everyone is going to bite your head off if you try to talk to them, but you still need to get over the fear of people. There are two ways to do this.

The first way is prayer. I know it sounds like a default answer, but don't mock it until you try it. At one point, I spent a little time each day for a week just begging for the courage to talk to strangers. That's what all the first Christians did in Acts 4:29. I just asked and asked for Jesus to give me the strength to get over my fear and do it. I didn't pray like I was ordering fast food. It wasn't a casual time. I really got desperate and begged because I realized that, day by day, my life was passing before my eyes. Just as Psalms 90:10 says:

> *The years of our life are seventy,*
> *or even by reason of strength eighty;*
> *yet their span is but toil and trouble;*
> *they are soon gone, and we fly away.*

Fast forward a week or so. *It actually worked.* It kind of alarmed me at first. Did the God who shook Mount Sinai actually hear me talking to Him? He must have, because I was talking to people that I used to be afraid of. Strangers or friends, it didn't matter to me.

Now, after talking with thousands of people, the fear level is almost gone. It's like I just don't care anymore. Do I still get nervous? Sure, but it's nothing like it was initially. I've gotten over that big roadblock of fear through desperate prayer.

The second way is to start fearing the right things. It's actually remembering who you should fear in the first place. We won't answer to people on Earth when we die. We will answer to the Judge of the Universe, the King of Israel. It is no lighthearted matter, so remembering who Jesus warned us to fear should keep our priorities straight. He used some strong words in Luke 12:4–9 when he said this:

> *I tell you, my friends,*
> *do not fear those who kill the body, and after that have*
> *nothing more that they can do.*
> *But I will warn you whom to fear: fear him who, after*
> *he has killed, has authority to cast into hell.*
> *Yes, I tell you, fear him! ...*
>
> *And I tell you,*
> *everyone who acknowledges me before men,*
> *the Son of Man also will acknowledge before the angels*
> *of God,*
> *but the one who denies me before men will be denied*
> *before the angels of God.*

Isn't it interesting that Jesus mentions not fearing people in the same breath He mentions acknowledging Him before men? I think it's because they go together. If you fear the Lord, at some point, you will take His command seriously to acknowledge Him before men and you will speak up. At some point, you should get to the edge of the cliff (so to speak) and tell someone about your Savior, no matter what the cost. Don't fear man. Fear the One who will acknowledge you before God the Father.

So, if you're scared, just remember that you're going to learn what to say right here in this book. After that, beg King Jesus for some help!

A Final Lesson: It's Not Only About the Lost

If there's a final valuable excuse eraser I've come across from sharing my faith with people, it would be that it isn't always about the lost. It's also about the people who come with me.

I try to take younger people along. They're excited to go because it's a challenge for them. Well, after I started bringing them along, I noticed something: I was talking with strangers and the people I brought with me were listening. They got to watch. If they were scared, they would just stay at a distance and pretend they didn't know me. That's fine with me. Over time, their bravery grew. They saw that they could probably do the same thing that I was doing. Before I knew it, they were telling me stories of people they were talking to about the gospel when I wasn't around.

Below is an actual e-mail I got from someone's parents:

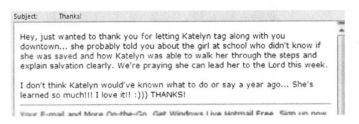

So, you might question whether sharing the gospel with strangers works or not. Maybe it's just working on different people than you thought.

CHAPTER FIVE

WHAT SHOULD I SAY?

What Should I Say?

The fruit of the righteous is a tree of life,
And he who wins souls is wise.[7]
~ Proverbs 11:30 ~

Just so you know, I know all about the Romans Road and the draw-the-cross-as-a-bridge-napkin drawing. I've seen all the methods. There's one problem: they're not very dynamic. They might be nice *if no one ever asks you a question.* The problem is that you end up talking to people, and to do that you need to know how to have a conversation and interact with them.

Let's get a few things set up in our minds first and then we're on our way to our first conversation about Jesus.

Hey, Watch Your Tone!

You know when you're at Chili's and you get up from the table and you go to the hostess and you say, "Excuse me, I'm sorry to bother you. Where are the restrooms?" That's the tone of voice you should use when you go up to someone and start talking to them about eternal things. You don't want to scare them and put them on the defensive right away. That never works. You want to win their ear for just a few minutes, and your tone of voice is important. So now you know that before you talk to *anyone,* always remember that you should use the same tone as when you ask where

---

7   New King James Version.

the bathroom is. Just relax. As long as you talk to people in a gentle and loving way, you'll be fine.

How Long Will This Take?

What we're about to discuss can take place in ten minutes or ten months. Sometimes I talk through these ideas with one person the first time I see them, and sometimes it takes a while to talk it through with a friend.

I'll give you an example. There was a friend of mine that I worked with whom I hadn't seen in a while. He was moving, so he wanted to meet up and have lunch. I didn't waste a lot of time, so I told him about my faith pretty early on in the conversation. I went through the main ideas that we'll go over here, and he actually wanted a book about what we talked about. I got him a book, gave it to him the next day, and he moved to Europe. This took a few minutes. Other conversations have gone on for months.

Was there anything similar about those conversations? Yes. Both of the conversations headed in the same direction. You will talk about the same kinds of ideas with everyone, no matter how long or how many times you talk with them.

Be Comfortable with Being Uncomfortable

I hear professional athletes say they still get nervous before they play in a big game. I hear musicians say the same thing about concerts. You know what's funny about it? They still go out there and do it. I still get nervous sometimes when I go share my faith with people, but I'm going to play through it. It's no different than what an athlete or a musician would do. Shouldn't we be just as brave as they are?

So, if you want to share the gospel, you have to be comfortable with being uncomfortable. I still misjudge situations and say the wrong thing. I still feel awkward sometimes when someone says something harsh back to me. Just the other day someone just walked away from me. He didn't even say anything! We started talking and he just walked away. I know that he wasn't rejecting me, but it felt that way. On the flip side of being nervous, feeling awkward, and getting rejected, you might see someone put their faith in Jesus. Sometimes the reward is much bigger than the feeling of nervousness or any rejection you might face.

Everyone I've ever known who started sharing the gospel had to be uncomfortable for the first few times. After that, they *always* end up telling me that it wasn't that hard. After they get over their initial fear, they're excited and ready to try it again. They would all tell you that you're missing out if you're not sharing your faith. I promise.

Rejection

You're going to get rejected. It's just part of the deal, but there's nothing to be scared of. Just know that some people aren't going to want to talk. But here's the thing to remember: you will also be very surprised. A lot of people you think won't want to talk to you actually will, and you never know who it'll be. I have been surprised so many times at the people who are *willing* to talk that it makes me feel bad about all the people I've walked by.

There was one time when I was right in the middle of a downtown area of a city with some friends and we started talking to four middle-aged men. They looked very serious and unfriendly. You would have never thought they would have wanted to talk about Jesus, of all things, but they were still listening twenty minutes later. One guy actually spoke up and said, "I'm actually Jewish, and you're telling me that Jesus is the Messiah and can forgive my sins?" They all ended up thanking us for the conversation. I was surprised.

I write that story to encourage you because there are other times when things won't work out so well. Just brush it off and remember what Jesus said in Matthew 5:11–12:

> *Blessed are you when others revile you and persecute you and utter all kinds of evil against you falsely **on my account**. Rejoice and be glad, for **your reward is great in heaven**, for so they persecuted the prophets who were before you.*

This means that rewards are coming your way when you get rejected. But even if someone rejects you, don't give up on the person right away. I've learned that when people are hesitant to talk, showing them love almost always opens their ears to listen to the gospel. I've written a special section on this called *Good Works: Don't Just Do Them, Use Them* at the end of this book.

There are even rewards in the kingdom for winning people to Jesus, so it's not a big deal if you get rejected a few times along the way. Look at what Daniel wrote:

> *And those who are wise shall shine like the brightness of the sky above, and those who turn many to righteousness, like the stars forever and ever.*[8]

Will you be one of the people Daniel was writing about who led many people to righteousness? If you're still alive, you've still got time. Now it's time to learn how to actually share your faith.

---

8 Daniel 12:3

Here Goes Nothing

The beginning of any conversation starts with one idea in your mind. It's a pretty simple if-then type of idea.

IF someone dies,
THEN what happens next?

Ask something along these lines to get this idea across to people:

"Hey, can I ask you a quick question?"

"Hey, we're out here asking people a few questions …"

Then …

"If you died, where do you think you would go?"

"What do you think of the afterlife?"

"Do you think there's an afterlife?"

"What are your thoughts on the afterlife?"

"Do you think anything happens to people when they die?"

All these questions focus around our if-then idea. When you die, what's next? Asking any of the above questions directs the conversation that way. The fun has begun.

I've learned that asking people about the "afterlife" is a great question. It's a non-religious and general question that piques people's curiosity. You're not in their face right away; you're just asking a general question. People do not get overly offended at this question. You could ask it of fifty people, and maybe one of them will bark at you. If someone gets offended because of this question, he will definitely be offended when you start to talk about heaven, hell, and (gulp) Jesus.

You Did It!

Finding the courage to ask that initial question is the biggest hurdle to get over. It doesn't matter if you've been friends for thirty seconds or thirty years. Trust me that it's the initial nervousness of talking to people about this that is so difficult.

Want to be like Paul? Get over this fear. It's scary and awkward; kind of like asking a girl out on a date in ninth grade. But you can do it. Try asking the person checking you out of the grocery store to see what he says. Don't feel any pressure to say anything more. Just act like you're trying to get his opinion on it. Once you get comfortable talking with people like this, the rest will be easy. Nothing will be hurt if you just try it a few times, will it?

Now for the next piece of valuable information.

Let Them Talk

You asked a total stranger (or maybe your uncle) something like what's written above. Now let him talk. Shut your mouth and listen. You will learn almost everything you need to know about someone's spiritual views by how he answers this question. You can gather most of the information you need to know in fifteen seconds.

When you let people talk after this initial question, you will get some great answers. Some people will say, "I'm going to heaven because I believe Jesus died and rose from the dead." Other answers will make you laugh. There's always the "spaceship is going to pick me up" guy. Some people will say, "I'm going straight to hell, I'm awful." Other people will say they're going to paradise because of the good things they've done. Let them talk and see what they think. For now, just keep your mouth zipped and say, "Oh okay." Nod your head and listen.

In a completely unrelated story, I was in Starbucks once and was *not* interested in the free coffee they were giving out. I didn't want any of it. The girl working there asked me if I wanted a free sample and I just said, "Oh no thanks. It'll probably just clutter up my house, I have so much …"

She politely interrupted and said, "Well, you can just take some, you know."

"No, it's okay," I replied.

She smiled and said, "You know this is our new instant coffee? It took ten years to design; people really like it. Here you go."

As I was mesmerized by her inability to let me throw her off course, she put the instant coffee in my hand. I ended up leaving Starbucks with a handful of instant coffee packets.

What's the point? She listened to me, but she kept displaying her passion for where she worked. She didn't get discouraged, give up, or lose her cool at all. ***And it actually got me to open up.*** Sharing the gospel is the same type of thing. Let people answer an initial question about life after death and be ready to just keep going. Don't give up. If they're not willing to talk, you'll know. If they're willing to listen, keep going! We'll show you what to do next.

WARNING! You might meet the "I don't think anything happens" guy.

There is one little problem you can run into here. While most people think there is life after death, there are the "nothing happens when you die" or "your body just goes into the ground" kind of answers. Some of these people will say that they don't think God exists. They might be skeptical about everything. Uh-oh; that wasn't what we planned for.

What should you do? You could say something like, "Well, Jesus said you're going to burn in hell!" I would suggest against it. Instead, you could just ask them about someone interesting who has died. Here's the million-dollar question:

What about Hitler?

Do you really think Hitler killed 6 million Jewish people and God overlooked all that after Hitler died? Almost 100 percent of people say no way. In fact, I've met people who initially said that nothing happens after death to then say that Hitler went to hell. I hadn't even said anything about him going to heaven or hell yet; I just asked about the afterlife. I think that it's just an instinctive response because someone as evil as Hitler had to pay for what he did. The normal guy on the street will agree and say that God should punish him for what he did.

I know what you're thinking: you're assuming they already believe there's a God, even though it didn't seem like it initially. First they said that they didn't think anything happens after death and then they changed. What's the deal with that?

Yes, I am assuming they think there's a God, even if they don't initially acknowledge it. Romans 1:21 tells me everything I need to know. It says that, "Although they knew God, they did not honor him as God or give thanks to him." So everyone *knows* there's a God, they just suppress the truth about Him. They might not know exactly who He is. They might not know that He's the God of Abraham and Isaac, but they know something is out there. When you ask someone this question about Hitler, it brings that to the surface without the person even knowing he's admitting it.

People who act like they don't think God exists (atheists) or they're just unsure (agnostics) can slip up here when you ask them about an extreme example like Hitler. This cuts through a lot of going back and forth about the evidence for God's existence. To the person who you're talking to, the evidence that *they* think God exists is what just slipped out of their mouth. Oops!

Side Note: The Great Switch

There is power in discussing things this way. There are people who have changed what they said they thought about God in fifteen seconds. You may not believe me, but don't doubt it until you try it.

In our Adolf Hitler example, people need to make a choice. Either they admit that what he did was wrong or they say it doesn't matter. When you ask them this, it stirs up the justice measuring stick in their brain, and most people will say that they think Hitler is in hell. This is what I call The Switch. Many of the things we'll go over in next section work this way. People will quickly admit something different than they did initially because you lovingly pressed the right button in their brain. They realize they said something that doesn't make much sense.

Well now, we've got a problem. If Hitler went to hell, what's the standard God should use to judge everyone else? What if Hitler only killed a million people? Would that be bad? What if he only killed one? Would God just let him into heaven for that? What about lying? Stealing?

People who say that Hitler just got away with all of that are rare. They probably aren't going to think they're all that bad if they don't think Hitler was. Do you really think they're going to talk about their own sin if they don't think Hitler had to answer for his? You should try to keep talking with them, but trust me that you won't find many people like this. If you do meet someone like this, you could mention some evidence for God's existence before you talk about the gospel. We will go over that in the section about evolution, so just keep reading.

At the Edge of the Cliff

Now you're at the same point with everyone: they all admit there's some kind of an afterlife. People might say they're going to heaven, hell, a spaceship, or they might say nothing as we just went over. The important thing is to get everyone to consider this question next:

What determines who goes where after we die?

Getting someone to ponder this one thing is important. The sad thing is that most people will say that they don't know. They might say something general about doing good things to get to heaven, but most people will have trouble giving you an answer on the spot. That's okay. Here's another question that helps people think about this:

Does everyone go to the same place?

People usually say no, which is a good answer. We're right on track and this is where the conversation gets very interesting.

The Answer

The answer you can offer usually surprises people: God doesn't determine someone's final destination based on their good deeds versus their bad ones. He decides based on whether they're innocent or guilty. The most loving thing you can do for someone is show them how this will actually happen.

Have You Ever Heard of Moses?

To show someone how God would determine if they were guilty or not, you just need to show them that they've sinned. The easiest way to do this is to look at Moses. I'll actually ask people here, "Have you ever heard of Moses?" It keeps their interest; most people have seen *The Ten Commandments* movie. I'll just get right into it and ask them, "Did you know God gave Moses His laws? Do you know what they are?"

It's important when you go through some of these laws with people that you avoid using ones that could be misunderstood. Don't ask them if they've broken the Sabbath. You're probably not going to meet a first-century rabbi who could discuss the meaning of the Sabbath in the Torah with you. Use your brain.

Out of the nine commandments we mentioned earlier, the six Commandments below are the easiest ones for people to understand. They are laws that everyone has broken in one way or another, so I usually gently go through a few with them. "One of them is not to lie; have you ever done that? I have." See what they say. Here are the other ones to discuss:

- **Do not commit adultery**—It's important to remember that Jesus explained more about this law and said that if you just look at someone else with lust, it's adultery in your heart.[9]

- **Do not lie**

- **Do not steal**

- **Have no gods before me**—Have you ever put anything before loving God in your priority list?

- **Honor your mother and father**—Is someone going to honestly say they've always done this?

---

9 Matthew 5:28

- **Do not use God's name in vain**—This is using God's name as a curse word. If you stubbed your toe on your bedpost and you said His name out loud in your anger, you have sinned.

You can go through these one at a time with people and see how they do. Just using these Commandments will show someone they have sinned against God. If they say they've never broken any of them, I'll usually tell them they're crazy and we both laugh. They know that isn't true.

This is where we get to the heart of the matter. Why? Because of this profound idea that you need to remember:

1. God is just.

2. Because of #1, he cannot overlook a crime when someone breaks one of His laws.

3. It would be unfair for God to forgive you for free.

So, if anyone has broken God's laws, he is guilty. And God can't just throw out someone's guilty record for free. We're going to talk about Jesus next, but before we do that we just need to remember a few quick points.

Quick Points to Remember

Finish Strong

It's important to remember to finish the right way when you go through these laws with someone. People have suggested asking someone if they are guilty or innocent. Don't even bother. I just ask them:

Well, wouldn't you be guilty?

The next obvious question is what happens when someone meets God with a guilty sin record. This leaves less wiggle room and gets right to the point, and this is where most people admit that they would go to hell.

It is important to lovingly make someone realize they deserve to go to hell. It's important for them to admit that they would be guilty and what that means for them. You should be gentle and loving, but showing someone this is important. Don't skip it.

I saw this work well a few summers ago. A close friend of mine did a summer sports camp for the residents of a poor apartment complex in our city. He said there would be tons of kids there who would be curious about the gospel. Sign me up. Well, I knew we would be there for the whole week, so I planned ahead. The first few days with these teenage guys were spent talking about what sin was. I was loving. I admitted to doing everything I asked them about, and they listened. After a few days, I said to them, "So, how can God just overlook all the things you guys admit that you've done?" They were so silent that it would have scared you. I let it marinate.

The next day came and I did the same thing. I said nothing about Jesus. I asked them as I left that night, "Hey, did you guys know that God did something so that all of your sins can be erased from your record?" A younger guy in the group yelled at me, "What is it! Come on, tell us!" Nope. I walked away and came back the next day.

Guess what? When I eventually got to Jesus, the punishment-taking substitute, it made sense to them. Some of them even told me later that they had gone home that night and asked Jesus to forgive them of their sins. I didn't pray with them, I didn't ask them to repeat a catch phrase, and I didn't tell them they needed a hole in their heart filled.

In a loving way, I just let the weight of sin point them to the fact that they needed a Savior.

Be Smart About It

If you ask someone if they've ever lied before (or any other sin) they might be hesitant to answer. They might say no because they're embarrassed or they honestly think they have never done it. But we all know everybody has lied before. The trick is getting someone to admit things like this.

The easiest way to get someone to talk about sin with you is to get close to their heart. I'll ask someone, "So if your boss told you he was going to pay you, and then he didn't, would you be upset?" Of course they would be upset. No one likes being lied to, but haven't we done the same thing? We've lied about things, regardless of what it was about. Using examples like this, where people would be upset if someone sinned against them, usually proves the point and helps them admit that sin is wrong.

Include Yourself

When you are talking about lying, adultery, putting other things before God, etc., it's important not to look self-righteous. I'll usually say, "Haven't you lied? I have." I'll throw a few of those before I only focus on them. Remember that you are talking to a person. They're not another notch in your belt of people you talked to about Jesus that day. You were guilty once too, and since you're sharing your faith with other people, have the humility to admit you were once in the same boat. I have found this to lower the walls of resistance when talking to people.

It also intrigues them. You're admitting to the same crimes they are, so people realize this conversation is going somewhere different than they expected. Why would someone talk to me about this and admit they've done the same things? They must have something more to tell me.

As a conversation goes on like this for five minutes or five months, you can ask them more pointed questions. If you go up to a random person on the street and tell them they've broken all of God's moral laws and they're in big trouble and they're such a sinner and ... they're going to shut up like a clam and not want to talk. After you're humble and win their ear, they will let you ask them if they have broken these laws and what that means if they have.

I am not saying you should let the person feel like they are all right with God because you've done the same things. You want people to feel uncomfortable with their sin. You want them to squirm and get defensive because that means they are being convicted. At the same time, you don't want to come across like the accuser of the universe. Paul said that he struggled with the war in his flesh in Romans 7, so it's only fair that when we are engaging people with these heavy truths that we're just as humble.

If They're Listening

Another thing to watch for is someone who is really paying attention. I've met tons of people who say things like, "I was just thinking about this death thing the other day." They will gladly hear you out. Other people will have eyes as big as softballs because they're just shocked someone would bring up such a pointed subject.

As backward as this will sound, if you notice that they're really listening to you, you need to convince them that they are in massive trouble. To do this, I just use an example here on Earth that people can understand. It actually helps elevate the importance of what Jesus did on the cross and in His resurrection.

Let's look at Iraq. Can you imagine what would have happened if you had broken all the laws in Saddam Hussein's kingdom—and then went off to meet him? He was a powerful ruler. Well, now look at the situation you're in: you've broken the laws of the Creator of the universe, and you're going to meet Him one day. As of right now, it's with a guilty record.

I used this example once with a few guys I was talking to and it worked perfectly. I said, "Can you imagine breaking every law in someone's kingdom and then going to meet the king? That'd be scary. Like ... oh, I don't know ... Saddam Hussein. What if you broke all the laws in Iraq then went to meet Saddam?" These two guys instantly laughed out loud. They couldn't hold it in. They said, "Yeah, that'd be scary because we're from Iraq!" The example I gave to them totally made sense.

Then I move things over to God. Imagine that you're not answering to a powerful ruler on earth, but the God who created the stars in the sky with the breath of His mouth. He killed 185,000 Assyrian troops in the book of Isaiah. He shook a mountain called Sinai. Imagine that.

The Ideal Ending

A conversation I had with an Indian guy from Clemson University is the best example of where a good conversation like this can lead. After going through some of the Commandments, I asked him if he thought he was guilty, and he said he was. I went on and asked him, "So what are you going to do?" That's a great question to ask someone here. Ask them what they think they should do. This guy asked the right question.

He said, *"I have no idea. What should I do?"*

This is exactly where you want someone to be. You want them to see themselves as guilty before God and question what in the world they should do next. And this is right where Jesus comes in.

Enter Jesus

So, you've started talking to someone using what we've already gone over here. Where does Jesus fit in and how can you talk about Him? Once we help other people realize what sin is and what God says about the punishment we all deserve, what Jesus accomplished makes much more sense. Remember, if God is just then He can't simply overlook anyone's sin. It doesn't matter how big or small it is.

Eraser

The reason Jesus died can be explained as the sin-record eraser. When Jesus died on the cross, he acted as a substitute for us. He took the punishment for our sins in our place. I emphasize to people that Jesus died so that all those who believe in Him will have their sin records erased. Deleted. Thrown out. It seems to hit home with people.

Once we understand what Jesus did on the cross, we need to be careful when we tell people what they need to do to have it applied to their own sins. I heard that a group of Muslims were once told by a preacher that they needed to "accept Jesus into their hearts." They walked away and didn't understand how a man could fit inside them. Go ahead and laugh out loud.

For someone to have what Jesus did applied to their own sin record and never be judged in hell for their sin again, they need to do two things:

Repent and Believe

Repentance is changing your mind and attitude toward sin. It doesn't mean clean up your life then come to Jesus. It means you realize your sin is wrong, you feel sorrowful over it, and you confess it to God. You turn from your sin to Jesus for forgiveness at the same time.

Faith means that we put our trust in Jesus for the forgiveness of all of our sins. We're simply trusting in this: the punishment He took on the cross and His resurrection three days later was the full payment for all of our sin.

Jesus told us to share these specific things with people in Luke 24:48:

> ... **repentance** and **forgiveness of sins** should be proclaimed in his name to all nations.

Paul says the same thing in Acts 20:21. Paul said that he was:

> ...testifying both to Jews and to Greeks of **repentance** toward God and of **faith** in our Lord Jesus Christ.

Repentance and faith are twin brothers. People don't repent of their sins and then believe in Jesus six months later. We need to acknowledge our sins before God and turn to Jesus for the forgiveness of them. They go together.

Notice that Jesus and Paul *never* tell anyone to "invite Christ into their life," "accept Jesus into their heart," "give their life to Christ," or "make Him Lord and Savior." They were clear on how to share the message. Confess your sins against God and believe in His Son. Repentance and faith are the two things Jesus and Paul stuck with, and we don't have editing rights here.

I was actually at the Salvation Army once when I met a man who worked there. I walked up to him and asked him, "Hey, can I ask you a question? Ever thought about what happens when you die?" He said he was raised in church and his name was actually Solomon. After explaining sin and the gospel to him, I told him that forgiveness means that your sin record with God is erased. God could only offer this because someone else took the punishment that was deserved. I shared with him that he needed to repent of his sins and put his faith in Jesus, just like we talked about earlier in this section. He looked me in the face in a quiet but honest way and said, "I have never had anyone explain it like that before. I've never really understood all this stuff. Thank you so much for talking to me about this. It's a really big deal."

At the End of the Road

You will get to a point when you're talking to people and you need to explain to them that Jesus requires a decision to be made. It's a yes or no thing. Don't be afraid to be clear on this point. You want to emphasize that they need to go to Jesus by themselves. You are not praying for them to God, and you're not saying a prayer for someone else to repeat. You're just pointing them to the One who can forgive their sin.

If you're friends, you can meet and talk a dozen more times about it if you want to. If they're a stranger, you can give him your phone number, get his e-mail address, or do whatever else you want to do. Just remember that this is a personal issue between that person and God, and you can only bring a person so far.

The Whole Conversation

In the ideal situation, you have gone over the following with someone:

1. What do you think about the afterlife?

2. Well, how does God decide who goes where when we die?

3. Suggest the answer to them. Since God decides our final destination through an innocent or guilty verdict, are you guilty right now? Look at the Ten Commandments with them.

4. Since you're guilty (just like I used to be), do you know the one specific thing God did to offer you a clean sin record and eternal life?

5. Since Jesus died and rose from the dead, and based on that alone, you can be completely forgiven of all your sin. You need to repent of your sin and put your trust in Jesus for the forgiveness of your sin. I had to do it too. Then you'll have eternal life, an innocent record with God, and a new heart with new desires. You'll never be judged for your sins again.

You don't have to repeat it exactly like this; this is just the general direction of the ideal conversation. After you talk with them, hopefully the person acts on their conviction. They might look to Jesus for the forgiveness of their sins right there, or it might take six months.

You should know that some people don't understand all this the first time around. I remember a time when I was talking about the gospel with a guy I had just met. After the second time we met, he told me that he didn't understand the depth of what Jesus actually did for sin. He was under the impression that doing good things would get him into heaven. It was much more personal to him then because he understood what Jesus actually did for him, but it took awhile to sink in.

A Final Question: What's the One Thing Holding You Back?

One thing that you want to leave someone with if they are open to listening is this: "Well, what's the one thing that's holding you back?" You'll be very surprised at the answers you'll hear. Sometimes they will say something completely unrelated to anything you talked about. That's a good thing because then you can address their question.

CHAPTER SIX

BUMPS IN THE ROAD

Bumps in the Road

I've seen different races and ages and genders say the *exact same thing* to the ideas we just went over. Word for word. For whatever reason, people love to make up questions and shield themselves when someone else talks about God-related topics. I don't want anyone to go through the frustration of having to think up answers to these problems that people bring up, so that's exactly what we're going to handle here.

It's not that big of a deal and you don't have to be a scholar. Don't worry. We all just need some railroad tracks to stay between when we're talking to someone and they ask a question. Once you learn all the typical questions that people ask and you know how to interact with them, your life gets much easier.

What About All That Evidence?

When I was in Israel once, I was privileged to go to a house church there. The pastor said something I will never forget: he reminded all the believers that the Israelites did not escape out of Egypt into the desert through the wisdom of Moses. They didn't break away from Pharaoh because Moses was a good negotiator. The Hebrew people broke out of slavery through the *power of God*. It's the same idea with the gospel because that's where our power is.

What we're going to go over will help you stay focused on talking about Jesus and what He did on the cross for sin (powerful) instead of arguing about something like evolution for hours at a time (not so powerful). People get saved when they repent of their sins and believe in the Son, so I'm not always worried about giving people long answers to problems they bring up. I want to get them to see what God did for them in the gospel.

Evidence and arguments are good, but they are like an air tank. If you're stuck at the bottom of the ocean and you only had one tank of air to get you to the top, you would use that air wisely. We need to do the same with all of our evidence. We should only use it when we need to.

Problem #1: God Will Send Someone to Hell for Lying? That's Ridiculous.

Most people think that lying or stealing is not a big deal. If you just do it once or twice (as if someone has only lied *once*), you shouldn't have to go to hell over it! The math looks something like this:

A finite number of sins on earth are **NOT EQUAL TO** *an infinitely long punishment in hell.*

How do sins during fifty years equal out to an eternal punishment? The math doesn't work out well, if you think about it. This is because we just think about it in the wrong way.

The problem is who our sins *are against*.[10] That's why the punishment is so severe. Just think about our Saddam Hussein example from before. If you called a random guy on a street in Iraq an idiot, he might get upset. If you called Saddam an idiot, you're in massive trouble. *Who* you offend determines your punishment, and our sin is offending God Almighty.

Sometimes I use the FBI. If someone doesn't think it's a big deal to sin against God, what about breaking laws that the FBI enforces? I'll throw this out there, "Hey, so if you broke just *one* law that the FBI enforces and they came knocking on your door, wouldn't you be scared out of your mind?" They usually agree. Then I just switch it over to God, like we talked about in the *If They're Listening* section. "Well, now we're talking about breaking the laws of the Creator of the universe … and you've done it *every day* of your life." Or what if you stole a cookie from an infant instead of a black bear? Wouldn't the consequences be different? You get the point. Same action, different consequences. It's important that people understand this or they will not understand why hell is reasonable.

---

10 This has been raised by people such as Jonathan Edwards.

Hard to Swallow

Even after you explain that it's who we're sinning against that makes the punishment so severe, people may still disagree. But it doesn't matter. At the end of the day, it's like that hard chemistry class in college: you don't get to grade your own final. You are questioned and graded how the teacher sees fit.

It's the same way with God. If we're guilty on Judgment Day, according to Him, we fail. If God says we deserve an eternal punishment, then that's the way it is. The chemistry teacher can give out questions and consequences that he sees fit, and God does the same thing.

It's Okay to Say It

I was flying home one time and met a teenage kid on the plane. I was reading something and he had headphones on, so I didn't try to share the gospel with him. I tried waiting it out because I didn't want to be rude. At the end of the plane ride, he said in a very humble voice, "Hey, what are you reading? Those papers caught my attention." That's what we call an "open door" (sense my sarcasm). I started talking to him. He was Catholic. It got to the point where we talked about what sin actually is. I could tell that as we gently discussed the issues, he started to get more curious. He wanted to hear more, so I told him exactly what I said above.

The amazing thing was that after I gave him the examples, he agreed with me. He understood why hell was reasonable. I then explained (lovingly) that he was storing up for himself an eternal punishment, and if he wanted that punishment diverted, he needed to repent of his sin and put his faith in Jesus *now*. I told him that God would wash away his sin record and he could have eternal life.

So, when someone tells you that it's unfair for God to send someone to hell for eternity, just use some examples we went over here. Then move on to telling them what Jesus did so that they can avoid that awful place.

Problem #2: Everyone Is a Sinner

This is my favorite reply. If you ask someone if they've ever lied, someone might say, "Yeah, but everyone's a sinner." They will agree with you pretty quickly they've stolen something, but everyone's done that, right? Somehow, everyone's innocent—because everyone is guilty? That doesn't make much sense. People seem to think that because everyone has lied, God grades on a curve. Since the highest grade on the physics final was a 71, the professor makes the 71 an A. God must be the same way. He must judge all people relative to *each other*. Everyone has sinned so it's no big deal.

I always try to cut this one off before it goes too far. I will point to myself and point to them (it could be five or six people) and say:

> *Yeah, but we're not talking about everyone*
> *else, we're just talking about us.*

It usually gets pretty quiet. Please trust me when I say that this one liner has **never** failed me. Regardless of the number of people you're talking to, this technique works well because people realize that they're making an excuse. Everyone knows if you killed someone and used the other-people-have-killed-people defense, you would get laughed at. CNN would pick it up and the video would be on YouTube.

That's all I say here. We're not talking about all these other people no one even knows. We're talking about us. Just you and me.

Why Do You Say *Us?*

It's important to say "us" instead of "you." Saying, "We're not talking about everyone else here, we're talking about YOU!" makes people think of that Uncle Sam poster I see in my nightmares. When you include yourself in the sin problem, it eliminates anyone thinking that you're the self-righteous Christian condemning all the dirty sinners.

It helps in refocusing the conversation between you and the person in front of you—and the gospel. You don't want to start debating all the "other" people in the world. This isn't a UN meeting. It's about our *personal* sin against God and the work Jesus did for our *personal sin record*.

So, the fact that "everyone has sinned" isn't the point. We have. Each of us. Keep it focused on that, and Jesus becomes a *personal* Savior.

Problem #3: I Think We're in Hell Right Now

As funny as it sounds, this response will actually come up. If you don't share your faith often, do not skip this question. People really do say this. I don't think they actually believe it, but it doesn't stop them from saying it to you.

The real problem is that if someone thinks we're living in hell right now, they're borrowing those ideas from the Bible. The Bible says that these are *eternal* places. Once you go there, it lasts forever. So this raises these questions:

If we're living in hell right now, why do we die? What happens then?

and

Okay, if we're all in hell right now, then who goes to heaven?

There's more. Sometimes, I just throw back the question:

That makes God pretty cruel then, doesn't it? Everyone is automatically born in hell?

Somehow, we're all living in hell on earth, and we showed up here by no fault of our own? That doesn't seem right.

I was talking to a guy one night about this exact problem. He just didn't want to admit that he deserved to go to hell. I quickly admitted that I did. He just didn't want to say it, so he defaulted to this typical reply. "Well, actually, I think we're in hell right now." I asked him, "Wait, so why do we die? Hell is supposed to last forever." He was stumped. It was that simple. Then I made sure I got back to the real issue: what happens when we really die and meet our Maker.

Problem #4: Oh Please, What if Christianity Isn't True?

If you start talking about life after death with someone, you might say something like, "I'm sure we both agree that no one would want to be wrong about any of this." Mr. Stranger will then say back to you, "Yeah, well, what if *you're wrong?!*"

Well, what if you are? What if Jesus is a joke and the Bible is a fairytale? It's a fair question.

To answer the question, I say, "I'd change my mind." If they find the body of Jesus, I'm out of here. If they find manuscripts of the New Testament that prove that Jesus is not the Son of God, I'm done. I could go on and on with what-ifs, but there's a problem. And this is exactly what I'll say to someone:

The reason I would never have to walk away is the evidence.

Here's where the conversation usually gets interesting. I can't even remember the number of people who have said, "What evidence?"

I would say that out of all the Jesus-sharing situations, this is where some hard facts are helpful. With other replies people give, it may not ever go in this direction. But with the reason that you'd never change *your* mind, you should explain some of the following:

> *There are **6,000 manuscripts** of the New Testament books in the original language. This is more than any other book in ancient history. Also, the copies we have of the originals are *earlier* than any other book in ancient history.[11]

---

11 More on this later, so stay tuned!

* The authors of the New Testament books were **eyewitnesses** to Jesus of Nazareth.

*All the copies of those books say 99 percent the same thing. The small percentage of difference is mostly in punctuation or differences in the way things were said in Greek.

*All the Apostles were murdered for their faith in Jesus. Just to make this point as heavy as possible: it was faith in a first-century Jewish man who claimed to be God, whom they saw rise from the dead, and who fulfilled prophecies about Himself from hundreds of years before He was physically born. If it's fake, then it sounds like hundreds of people were insane *all at the same time about the same person.* People don't usually hallucinate well in groups.

*Where's His body? Jesus of Nazareth is one of the most famous people who ever walked the earth. One of the main tenets of His followers is that He physically rose from the dead. If this didn't happen, where is His body? It would have been pretty easy for the Roman or Jewish leaders to squash this hoax. All they had to do was go get Him out of the grave and show Him to everyone!

I was talking to a guy my age once and I brought up this last one. I didn't go into anything extremely detailed where he could get confused. I just said to him, "The big problem is finding His body. Where did He go? They could have gotten rid of Christianity in ten minutes." He agreed with me that it was a good point.

There was another time when I was in a bookstore checkout line and I tried to talk to an older man behind the counter. We got to God-related things and the afterlife. With no hesitation, he told me, "Look, the Bible was written by a bunch of illiterate sheep herders 2,000 years ago. And by the way, a man in a huge boat escaped a big flood?! Give me a break." If I hadn't known any of the things I just went over and he said this, my pulse would have jumped. It can be uncomfortable—but not this time.

I took thirty seconds and went through exactly what I said above, and he completely changed his mind! He said, "Wait, what? I didn't know this. Say some of that again?" I went on to explain to him why there are plenty of good reasons to trust what the Old and New Testaments say, especially about life after death.

It's important to notice that you're not just throwing out evidence to win an argument. You're telling someone else why *you* wouldn't change *your* mind. It fascinates people when you can actually answer. I promise you that this is enough information for most people you meet to say, "Wow, I didn't know any of that." Sometimes, they just stand there convicted because they realize they just ventured into previously uncharted waters.

You need to remember one other important thing: giving someone facts and evidence can lead to certain conclusions. You can prove God exists and the Bible is reliable. Big deal. I can prove to you there's a moon that floats around our planet. When sharing this kind of factual information with someone, ***make sure*** you get back to the gospel. Make sure that the person understands that while you are giving them evidence that Jesus was a real person and that He really rose from the dead, you also can't leave Him on the shelf. You need to do something with Him. You need to repent of your sins and put your faith in Him or you're going to hell. No one is judging anyone else here because I was in the same boat.

If you want more in-depth information on evidence that supports the Bible, check out the helpful index in the back of the book. We list all kinds of other sources for you to read.

Problem #5: You've Never Been to Heaven or Hell, so You Can't Tell Me about It!

A lot of people will bring this one up. They will say something like, "Well, no one has been to hell and back to tell us about it, so we can't know anything about it." It's funny when people say this because they're actually right. I've never been to heaven, and I'll never go to hell. Outer darkness where people are gnashing their teeth? I'll pass.

It seems like we're out of options here. Unless, of course, we ask the person the same kind of question. Ask him if he has ever been to Afghanistan. Maybe Alaska? No? How do you know Afghanistan is even a real place? Sure, people have told you about it. Maybe you've seen a map or a TV show about it. The problem I throw back at the person is this:

You've never been there either.

We all know that there are camera tricks and maps that have been wrong. You really just trust someone else to tell you about these places; you're doing the same thing that you're accusing me of. I trust what the authors of the Bible tell me about life after death. You trust someone else to tell you about Afghanistan or Alaska.

Now, there are good reasons to think Afghanistan is a real place, and there are plenty of reasons we can trust what the Old and New Testaments tell us. These were all the reasons from the last section. If you want more, here is something interesting about the Old Testament:

> *The Dead Sea Scrolls. These were copies of the Old Testament books found in an area called Qumran. It's located at the northern end of the Dead Sea. Since these were copies of the Old Testament from before Jesus was born, we know the prophecies about Him weren't "written in" later:

Isaiah 7:14—The Messiah will be born of a virgin.

Isaiah 53—The Messiah will have the iniquity of us all laid on Him, and he will take the sin punishment for His people.

Daniel 9:24–27—Daniel predicted, to the exact day, when Jesus would ride into Jerusalem on a donkey and then die. Daniel said this would happen exactly 483 years after the command to rebuild Jerusalem was given. Check it out for yourself.

Micah 5:2—The Messiah would be born in Bethlehem.

Genesis 49:10—The Messiah would be from the tribe of Judah.

2 Samuel 7:12—The Messiah would be related to King David.

Psalm 22:16—The Messiah would be pierced in His hands and feet.

Zechariah 9:9—The Messiah will come into Jerusalem while riding on a donkey.

Who else in history has ever fulfilled these things other than Jesus of Nazareth? We know from the Dead Sea Scrolls that these things were predicted before Jesus showed up in the manger! By now, most people don't know what to say. They're kind of shocked. It's a great way to get back to the gospel, because now you have some backup and no one can accuse you of being a lunatic. They trust maps that tell them about Alaska, and you have good reasons to trust a book that tells you about life after death.

Problem #6: The Bible Was Written by Man, and We Don't Even Have the Originals!

If you don't know a lot about how the books in the Bible were initially written, a quick overview goes something like this. The Bible was written over a 1500 year period, mostly in Hebrew and Greek.

The originals were handwritten. They were copied by hand thousands of times, and we have thousands of the copies. The amazing thing is that through all that time, the copies remain miraculously similar and any differences don't affect anything significant. The copy of Isaiah that we have from the Dead Sea Scrolls is a thousand years younger than the copy we had before that, and they basically match word for word. But they were written and copied by *men*.

I had a guy bring this up once. He was sitting on a concrete wall a few feet high and seemed pretty bright. He got to a point and admitted that he's stuck on this one thing: the Bible was written by man. Even worse, the original copies of the Biblical books were handwritten. Uh oh! When people hear this, they usually write the Bible off right away without thinking through it.

I figured I would ask him the same question I've asked other people:

Really? Isn't that just like Darwin's notes?

He actually laughed out loud because he knew he was busted. Once he realized that Darwin's notes were handwritten and he was only reading a copy of them, he didn't have much to complain about when it came to the Bible. You can actually look at pictures of Darwin's notes if you go to *www.darwin-online.org.uk*. The funny thing is, you can barely even read them.

You see, most books that have anything to do with God (or the lack of Him) have handwritten originals. The Quran was handwritten. Darwin's notes were handwritten. The typewriter wasn't even invented until the late 1800s! Are you really telling me any thoughts on God before the 1800s are wrong because they were handwritten? That means that 99 percent or so of the world's population has beliefs that are false.

We may not have the originals of the New Testament books, but do you really think anyone has read through all the originals of other books about what they believe? Having or not having the originals must not be that big of a deal. Otherwise, everyone would be fighting over the originals of every book on the shelf. We would all ask for the originals at the bookstore instead of buying a copy.

To have a little fun and make the case even worse, there were decades that went by when Darwin's private notes were only available to scholars at the Cambridge University Library. The only way anyone else could have read them was to read—you guessed it—copies.

This shows how funny it is when people bring this up. We all know that we trust other people to copy things for us. As you might remember from previous sections, there are plenty of reasons we can trust the New Testament authors and the people who copied those books. Being handwritten and hand copied doesn't make a book untrue. Not having the originals to read doesn't make it untrue either.

This is usually all you need to bring up. The guy in the story where I used this idea was startled because he had the rug pulled out from under him. He was happy to listen to the rest of the gospel.

Problem #7: There Are so Many "Interpretations" and "Translations" of the Bible

This question goes right along with the last one. People don't understand how the Bible was put together; they watch one show on the History Channel with scholars who aren't in the Jesus fan club, and their mind is poisoned.

People use the word "interpretations" and "translations" together, even though the words mean two different things. I have no idea why people do this, but I guess it makes the Bible look really bad if you use more than one fancy word in a sentence.

> An *interpretation* of something involves providing what you think a statement means. "Sally jumped high" is something we could interpret. Well, how high? Did she jump repeatedly? How we interpret that would be communicating what it means.

> A *translation* is when you take something in one language and transform the message into a new language. You obviously try to preserve the original meaning from language number one to language number two.

Translations

There are **not** a million different "translations" of the Bible in the way that people think. This is an example of what people think happened:

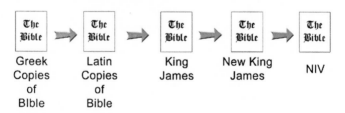

Greek Copies of Bible → Latin Copies of Bible → King James → New King James → NIV

Since it's been *translated* thousands of times, it must be full of errors. It supposedly went through different languages thousands of times. Back and forth, from English to Greek to Hebrew or whatever else anyone thinks. How in the world could it be reliable?

Well, that's not what happened. People in biblical times copied the originals of the books of the bible in their original language, and today we have thousands of those copies. We can look at all the manuscripts and see how carefully they've been preserved. As an example, when we look at all the copies that we have of the New Testament in Greek, they are 99 percent similar.[12] No one is hiding anything here because you can even look up pictures of these ancient copies on the internet.

When the Bible is translated, it comes from this collection of Hebrew and Greek copies. Don't forget that with the New Testament, we have the most and earliest copies of the Greek manuscripts when compared with *any other book* from ancient history.[13]

As an example, the New American Standard Bible is **not** translated from the King James Bible. This is actually what the translators do:

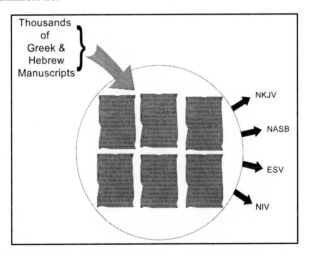

---

12 There are many books on this subject. Check out the appendix for good books on this.

13 See p.226 of *I Don't Have Enough Faith to Be an Atheist* by Norman Geisler for a helpful chart.

Versions of the Bible are translated into their language (i.e. English) from these copies in the original language. The different translations of the Bible are **not** translated from each other, but each new translation goes back to these Greek and Hebrew manuscripts.

When someone brings this up, you just need to ask the person if they're familiar with this. If not, give them these simple examples. It will be news to most of the people you meet, but just remember that the good news is not that the Bible is reliable: it's what's actually written down inside of it.

Interpretations

People will also say that there are so many "interpretations" of what's in the Bible. They'll throw things your way that sound like, "It's all up to your interpretation." This can be confusing if you don't know how to discuss it.

The best way to deal with this is to bring up something very direct and ask if there are different ways to "interpret" it. I love Isaiah 44:6:

I am the first and I am the last; besides me there is no god.

Another good one is Acts 4:12:

And there is salvation in no one else, for there is no other name under heaven given among men by which we must be saved.

Are there really a million different ways to interpret these verses? What about:

For there is one God, and there is one mediator between God and men, the man Christ Jesus.[14]

---

14 1 Timothy 2:5

I'm sure you get the point: there really aren't a million ways to "interpret" these verses. So the next time someone says that there are so many "interpretations" of the Bible, just ask them about one of these verses and see what they say.

I was actually talking about this exact issue with someone one Saturday morning. She wanted to meet up and talk about the Bible. I was happy to do it. She ended up telling me that so much of the Bible is open to interpretation, so we couldn't even know if there was even only one God. I opened my Bible to Isaiah 44:6 and asked her if the God of Israel was confused. She did not say *a word*. She didn't know that was in there! The great news is, we got to talk about the gospel after that, and later on in her life, she actually got saved. She called to tell me about it, and I was obviously excited for her. Jesus is mighty to save, proven true yet again.

Problem #8: Who Says the Bible Is True anyway?

By now, you're probably starting to catch on. Some of these questions don't really require detailed answers. But what if someone asks you a very direct question like this one? If you want to, you can give them some evidence we talked about before, but this question is a little different. You most likely won't need to say much here.

Why not? Because when someone objects to the Bible being true, you just need to throw a friendly question back their way:

Have you read the whole thing?

Now, most Christians haven't read the whole thing cover to cover. Why would an unbeliever? People with an open heart who read the Old and New Testament *usually* end up coming out the other end believing in Jesus. I just assume that someone who says this hasn't even read it all.

I'll go on just like I did above:

How do you know it's not true if you haven't even read it?

It is pretty unfair to say a book is untrue if you haven't even read the whole thing yourself. Now, pointing this out does two things:

1. It gives you the opportunity to ask them if they would try reading it sometime. Give them a Bible when you get the chance. God can work with that. That's how I came to put my faith in Jesus: I just read the book.

2. It gives you the chance to ask a great question: "Well, what do you think the main message of the Bible is?" People will say, "Be a better

person" or "Improve your life." Nope. It's about forgiveness of sins through faith in Jesus. Well, now you have the chance to give them the good news they've never heard.

Problem #9: What if Someone Never Hears About Jesus?

I just saw a video of a famous talk show host. She was asking the guest about people who never hear about Jesus. She said, "What about the man in Tibet, before there were TVs and radios. This man lived a *good* life ..." and that's when I turned it off. That's the point where the world always goes wrong. No one has lived a good life. We've all sinned and rebelled against God, so let's make sure we all understand that ahead of time. The Tibetan man wouldn't have to worry about hearing about Jesus if he was actually good in God's eyes. It's the same with all of us.

Before we get to the best question to ask someone, just stop and think for a second. Your new friend is hearing about Jesus from you when they bring up this problem of other people hearing about Jesus. You would think they would at least care about themselves first! If Jesus offers forgiveness of sins, why worry about a man in Tibet before you worry about yourself? I'll even gently ask people why they would be so concerned about someone that they don't even know.

Now, when someone brings this up, you *could* say, "Well, everyone who doesn't hear about Jesus is going to hell forever!" Bad idea. A better option is to ask them this simple question:

> *Do you know someone who went to hell who didn't hear about Jesus?*

What a ridiculous question! It works, though. If they say yes, that means they know there's a place of eternal torment they can avoid through believing the gospel. If they knew this before they met you, why wouldn't they be believers already?

If they say that they don't know anyone in this situation, then the obvious question is, "Okay, well then who are you so worried about?" This whole idea just makes one simple point: most people don't care about other people hearing about Jesus. It gently illustrates that they're trying to find a way out of this faith-in-Jesus-or-else situation.

For whatever reason, this question you can ask people stumps them. They usually drop the issue altogether. That's good, because I don't want to talk about it. I care about the person I'm talking to at the moment, not people halfway around the world. I want the person in front of me to worry about *their own* final destination. Then we're right back to the gospel again.

Sometimes they might want more. Maybe you didn't deliver the line like a young George Clooney. I always say:

> *Okay, but what if someone doesn't hear about Buddha? They'll never be enlightened.*
>
> *What if someone doesn't hear about Allah? They'll never even have a shot at paradise.*

Hopefully they see the point. The issue that they brought up about Jesus is the same with every other belief system as well. I just ask people that since they're all different:

> *No one would want to be wrong about this, would they?*

I've had people look right at me and say, "Oh man, that's a good point. I don't want to be wrong." You've cleared their mind from all the people-in-faraway-lands smoke screen. Now you're right back to talking about eternal life through Jesus the God man.

As I hope you can see, the trick with a touchy question like this is not to answer it. It's supercharged and loaded with land mines. Everyone listening is chomping at the bit, waiting for you to condemn the millions who haven't heard about Jesus. Let God do the judging; you try to get them to the cross.

Problem #10: No One Can Be Sure He's Going to Heaven.

People will usually say this because they think you are arrogant for talking about something like this with any degree of certainty. You could say, "I *am* sure! I'm going to heaven and you're not!" It sounds funny, but some people come across that way. Please don't say that. Always try to point to the gospel:

Well I am ... but it's not because I'm a good guy.

This one quickly piques people's curiosity. I've had small groups of people gathered around to listen after dropping that one. I actually had a guy say, "Wait, what? Why else would you be going to heaven?" This works because you're not bragging about yourself. You're not judging anyone else. You don't sound "religious."

There's another thing you need to remember here. You *always* want to display this idea:

Listen, I'm not telling you about me, I'm just trying to point you to someone else.

The point is to defuse any tension that comes with talking about your faith. It refocuses what you're talking about to what Jesus did on the cross for us. Trust me that that's where you want to stay.

One time I was talking to a girl as I was walking out of a store. We got to talking about this, and I asked her during our talk, "Do you think there's a difference between people who act more 'religious' than you and people who try to point you to someone else like Jesus?" Her eyes got really focused and she said, "Oh, absolutely. That's the problem with most Christians." Ouch!

You can come to an awkward moment with people, especially friends, whenever you talk about these things. They come to realize that you think that *they* are going to hell, but *you* won't be there with them. That's why it's important to push all the attention away from you. You want them to look right at Jesus and understand that He can save them from their sin and its eternal consequences. It's between them and Jesus. You're not the missing fourth member of the Trinity, so make sure they understand that you don't think you are.

Problem #11: God Could Never Forgive Me of All the Wrong I've Done.

Yes, believe it or not it's true: some people think they've done too much wrong for anyone (even God) to wipe their record clean and forgive them. They may have had an abortion, or they might have been in a war overseas and have a heavy conscience about some things they've been involved in.

I met a kid who had this problem while we were out sharing the gospel one night. He told me that he had been to jail a few times. You could tell he was hurting. With someone like this, you don't need to beat them up anymore. He knew he was bad and in trouble. He had been to jail!

With someone like this, you should use examples of *really wicked* people that God has been merciful to. Moses and Paul are great ones because they were both murderers, and they are the exact people I used when I talked to this guy who had been to jail.

Moses killed a guy that was beating up one of the other Hebrews and then buried him in the sand.[15] By the sounds of that, you probably wouldn't want him running your preschool. Before Paul was a follower of Jesus, his name was Saul. Here's a snapshot of his pre-Jesus life:

> *And the witnesses laid down their garments at the feet of a young man named Saul.*

> *…And Saul approved of his execution*

> *…Saul was ravaging the church, and entering house after house,*

---

15 Exodus 2:12

> *he dragged off men and women and committed them to prison.*[16]

In another place, Paul describes his sin before he believed in Jesus. Then, he describes the forgiveness of sins he received afterward. Look what he says in 1 Timothy 1:13-14:

> *...though formerly I was a blasphemer, persecutor, and insolent opponent.*
>
> *But I received mercy because I had acted ignorantly in unbelief,*
>
> *and the grace of our Lord overflowed for me*
>
> *with the faith and love that are in Christ Jesus.*

Paul was in charge of murdering and imprisoning both men and women because of his zeal to defend his branch of Judaism. The great thing about using Paul as an example is that once he put his faith in Jesus, God completely forgave his sin. Now that's a good story to share with someone. Don't let *anything* that person has done in the past stop them from coming to the Lord Jesus, no matter what they've done.

---

16 Acts 7:58, 8:1, 8:3

Problem #12: Well That's Good for You, but It's Not True for Everyone Else.

I know that there are plenty of books on how to defend Christianity and that there's a huge culture war over truth and all these types of things. But sometimes, when it would be better to keep things simple, we make things way too complex.

For this problem, we *could* go into a big, long definition of absolute truth and any other fancy terms you want to use. The average person will get lost (and bored) when you do this. I just use an example:

> *Let's say I have exactly a thousand dollars in my bank account and you didn't know that. Isn't it true that it's still there?*
>
> *What if you don't believe it's there?*
>
> *What if you don't even know about it?*
>
> *Does that change anything?*

This shows that if something is true, it's true *whether someone knows about it or not.* And it's about money, which people love to talk about. Even if someone didn't know that I had a thousand dollars in my bank account, it's still there. If all my friends didn't believe me, it wouldn't make a bit of difference. The hardest part for people to swallow is this: it is also true for everyone. If there is exactly a thousand dollars in my bank account, it's true *for everyone that it's there.* It doesn't matter if they acknowledge it or not.

Now we come face to face with a huge problem. Just like there isn't any room for differing opinions on the amount of money in my bank account, Jesus didn't leave any room for confusion when He talked about Himself. He made it clear that faith in Him was the only way to heaven, and it's true for everyone whether they believe it or not:

John 3:36

Whoever believes in the Son has eternal life; whoever does not obey the Son shall not see life, but the wrath of God remains on him.

John 8:24

Unless you believe that I am he you will die in your sins.

John 14:7

Jesus said to him, "I am the way, and the truth, and the life. No one comes to the Father except through me."

Well, these clear statements are in the Scriptures whether anyone knows it or not (just like the example of the thousand dollars in my bank account). They're sitting out there and the world is left with a decision. Either you take Jesus at His word or you don't. As hard as it is to accept, there's no "Jesus and my other religion," because Jesus doesn't allow for that. You either take Him or leave Him.

Although an example like using your bank account might sound too simple, it keeps people's attention and clearly makes your point. It's easier to stick with the gospel this way.

Problem #13: Well, All the World Religions "Teach the Same Things."

This question might seem like the last one, but it's not. We actually need to handle this question a little differently. Stick with me here.

I have heard thousands of people say that all the world religions are just different expressions of the same God. They might believe there's only one God, but there are different ways to express a relationship with Him. Sigh.

If you ever share your faith with anyone, you are going to meet people who pull out this every-other-religion card. Most of the time, they're really thinking that there is no way only one religion could be right; *therefore, they're all pretty much the same.* It's an easy way out, if you think about it.

There's one example I use when people say this. It works because it is obvious and easy to understand. You just need to compare what Christians and Muslims believe about the resurrection of Jesus. This is what Paul said about it:

> *If Christ has not been raised, then our preaching is in vain and your faith is in vain.*[17]

Just so you can see how clear the Bible is, take a look for yourself:

Matthew 28:5–6:
*I know that you seek Jesus who was crucified. He is not here, for **he has risen**, as he said. Come, see the place where he lay.*

---

17 1 Corinthians 15:14

Acts 2:23–24:

This Jesus, delivered up according to the definite plan and foreknowledge of God, you crucified and killed by the hands of lawless men. **God raised him up,** *loosing the pangs of death …*

Romans 1:4:

*… and was declared to be the Son of God in power according to the Spirit of holiness by **his resurrection from the dead,** Jesus Christ our Lord …*

1 Peter 1:3:

*According to his great mercy, he has caused us to be born again to a living hope through **the resurrection of Jesus Christ from the dead** …*

What's the big fuss about? Well, any other way and you have a dead Savior. You have the God-man who couldn't conquer death but who offered people eternal life. It just doesn't work. Instead, Jesus died and rose from the dead so that we can be forgiven of our sin once we believe. Not because we're good, not because we did good things, but because of the completed work of a substitute. It was Jesus on the cross and then Jesus walking around three days later. No resurrection, no Messiah Jesus. No forgiveness of sins.

Then we take a big turn.

We have the Quran. While I have had Muslim friends, and I love them dearly, this is something we disagree on because the Quran says that Jesus never died. It says He was not crucified. Muslims think someone else was up there on the cross dying. It goes on to say that Allah took him up into heaven himself. You can find this in Surah 4:157–158 of the Quran.

Put all those hostile feelings and politics aside. Deep breath. The only point being made here is that *everyone can't be right.* Christians and Muslims make up billions of people who live on the planet, but we disagree on a huge point in our beliefs.

Regardless to whom you're talking, this example works well. I'll talk for a second with someone on how the New Testament says Jesus died and rose again. After I mention the resurrection, I'll jump over to the Quran and point out that it says the exact opposite. Don't worry, people are not overly offended when you mention the Quran along with the Bible. I know what you're thinking.

I can't tell you how many people I've seen just stand in front of me silently. They may not have known that two of the main world religions were that different.

I brought a Jewish friend of mine out with me one night to go talk with some people. We came across a group of eight or so young Muslim guys. It was the Gentile, his Jewish friend, and eight Muslims. Diversity at its finest. They were having fun talking to us about Jesus; they had heard about Him in the Quran. For whatever reason, they thought all the religions of the world were kind of the same. We're all "children of God." I just used this simple example and asked them why the Quran says that Jesus wasn't crucified, but the New Testament says that He was. How can those be the same? Well, one of the guys who had been talking just shut his mouth. Another younger guy nudged his friend and told him to be quiet, because they seemed like they didn't know what they were talking about anymore!

Conclusion

You should know that this example has worked in all different situations, Muslim or not. People realize that this is a massive difference and that all religions cannot be correct. Use it when you can, and then get right back to talking about the forgiveness of sins that only Jesus offers.

Problem #14: A Lot of People Have Had Followers Like Jesus.

There was a guy named David Koresh. He lived in Texas in the 1990s and claimed to be a prophet. He had many "followers." The FBI ended up raiding the compound in which more than sixty people were living. Many of them ended up dying.

This kind of situation has happened many times before and after Jesus of Nazareth. So, aren't the followers of Jesus just the same kind of thing? You have some guy who claims to be a prophet (even though Jesus claimed to be God). That person has some followers. They die for their cause. Big deal.

A lot of people try to lump Jesus in with all the other cult leaders. It doesn't bother me when they do because I know exactly where I can go with this one:

*The disciples followed Jesus again **after** he rose from the dead.*

In Mark 14:27, Jesus tells the disciples they'll leave Him when He goes to get crucified and die. If you skip ahead to Mark 14:50, they all left Jesus and went away. All the disciples ditched Jesus, and He went to die alone.

The apostles started their ministry *after* Jesus died and rose from the dead. They didn't just blindly follow a first-century Jewish man into a suicide mission. They left Him and then came back to follow Him after He rose. As we asked before, where's His tomb? Where's His body? All these people followed Him after they said they saw Him alive from the dead; twenty centuries have passed and He's still missing in action.[18] I'll actually point this out to people and ask them:

You're telling me the most famous man in history supposedly rose from the dead and His doubters still can't find Him?

It seems like this would be pretty easy to disprove. The doubters at the time could have just dug up His body or could have shown everyone where He was still buried. Nothing like that is ever recorded in history. To make it even more convincing, the tomb that fits the first century description of where Jesus was buried near the hill of Golgotha is amazingly empty.

Remember that a lot of people have had followers. But they all followed their "leader" before he died and rose from the dead. That's a big difference.

---

18 There's very good historical evidence for the resurrection. See the index in the back of this book for more books to read that can help you here.

Problem #15: I've Done a Lot of Good Things.

This is the typical way that most people think. All world religions except Christianity work this way. The math for this one works out like this:

*A person does more good things than bad **EQUALS**
they're right with God and they go to heaven.*

The Old and New Testaments say something completely different. Let's use an example to handle this one quickly so that you can make your point with someone you're talking to:

*If someone kills three people and then saves four
people from a burning house, does that make
that person okay on the murder charges?*

Most people agree that that wouldn't work. The good things would not outweigh the bad. Let's make it more personal. Let's say someone kills your family and you're at the trial. Then, the murderer mentions all the people that he saved from death that week, and the judge lets him go. After all, he did more good than bad, right?

It's a pretty simple example but very powerful. Now the person understands that doing good things has nothing to do with being forgiven of a crime. This ultimately helps someone realize that doing good things won't help their sin record with God either.

Other Problems with This Idea

There are other problems with the idea of getting into heaven when we die because of our good works. The first one is **memory**. How can you remember what you've done right or wrong in the last thirty days? Three hundred days? Three thousand days? In all honesty, you can't. You have no assurance of anything in the afterlife if you think that you get into heaven through God balancing out your good and bad works. You should be nervous!

Another problem is the unique situation that all your good and bad deeds **are equal**. What if your good and bad deeds are exactly the same? People will say, "Oh well, then it's just up to God." Well that's not fair. I thought you were judged based on the wrong and right that *you've done*. God is just going to assign eternal damnation or eternal life to someone through His choice? One person has equal good and bad works, and they get into heaven. The next guy is in the same situation, and God decides to send him to hell. That's insane. That would be like a judge handing out arbitrary punishments for the same exact crime.

What's the Point?

The main problem with the idea that good and bad deeds determine your final destination with God is this:

> *It's not about comparing the good deeds versus bad; the problem is the sin on your record.*

It's the fact that you've done wrong, you've sinned, and aside from any good you've done, the bad deeds have to be dealt with somehow. A fine has to be paid, or they remain in your file.

I was standing outside of a restaurant one night and saw two guys waiting for some friends. I walked up to them and asked them what they thought about life after death. They agreed that there had to be something out there and that there must be a god. Eventually, we got to the point where I said, "Okay, so how would God decide who goes to heaven or hell?" One guy said, "I guess if you do more good than bad." I gave him the example we went over about killing three people and then saving four and he told me right away, "That makes more sense. I guess I was wrong." Then I got to explain what Jesus did in His death to deal with our sin problem.

Problem #16: There Are "So Many" Contradictions in the Bible.

If you come across someone who tells you there are a lot of contradictions in the Bible, it will most likely make you very defensive. You'll want to just yell at them, "No there's not!" Don't do that. You're just getting nervous because, well, there are a lot of verses they could pick from. Yikes.

Don't panic. The first thing you should do here is ask them:

Could you name one?

Name for me a legitimate contradiction in the Old or New Testament. Go from there. See if someone can name the chapter and verse of some contradiction. If they can't, it's kind of useless to talk about one. How do we even know where to find what you're talking about, Mr. Bible Objector?

This happens when people see a show on the Discovery Channel or read *The Da Vinci Code* and never check things out for themselves. But just like pigs might fly someday, people might name chapters and verses that contradict each other. You just need to understand the basics of how to handle this. Stick with me here.

There are a few common ones that people bring up. The death of Judas and the angels at the tomb of Jesus are both popular. It will just take a few seconds to go over these. It will help you to start thinking about how to answer these types of questions in the rare case that they come up.

Judas Dying

In Matthew 27:5, Judas hung himself. In Acts 1:18, Judas falls headlong and all his guts fall out. Those two descriptions seem to contradict each other unless you stop and think for a second.

What if he hung himself and then fell? Many scholars think that Judas hung himself on the edge of a cliff near the Valley of Hinnom. He could have hung himself, fallen, and split open. Not a big deal.

Angels at the Tomb

Mark 16:5 says there was one angel "on the right." John 20:12 and Luke 24:4 say that there were two angels at the tomb. Hmm. The first thing to notice in these passages is that it never says there was *only* one angel. Mark could have been talking about one of the angels that were there without mentioning all of them. It would be like talking to your friend about a football game without mentioning everyone else in the crowd.[19]

Conclusion

As you can see, many contradictions can be explained quickly. Just think about when the events took place (the two Judas hanging stories) or what the authors are including or excluding. (Did they use the words *only* to exclude all the other options?)

No need to worry, because most of the time, no one can name the places in the Bible where these things happen. If someone does get detailed with you, just look at our index in the back for places to get more advanced help, and get back to that person. It's okay if you don't know everything.

---

19 There are very detailed explanations of these potential contradictions. See our index in the back for books to check out on the subject.

Problem #17: I Don't Like When People Push Their Religion on Me.

I was in the mall right after Christmas one year, and I sat down next to an older guy. He was by himself, so I asked him if he was waiting for his wife. He laughed and told me he was waiting for her to finish shopping. He had spent all day sitting around in the mall. Yawn. I asked him how he spent Christmas and if he went to a church service. He said yes but he was uninterested. I asked him what he thought about all that "church stuff" and he said, "To each his own … I just don't like when people push their religion on me."

Shut down. If I share the gospel with him, I'll be doing exactly what he says he hates. That won't work. With people who act like this, it's important to try to find out some more about them. Ask anything general:

What religion did someone push on you?

or

Oh, what did they say?

The point of asking them this is to see if they're bluffing. Has this really happened to them and they've had a bad experience?

I'm actually going to have coffee with someone tomorrow morning who said that she has had bad experiences with church people. Understood. I can only guess the things they said and how they said them. Other people, however, haven't had bad experiences with Christians. They just don't like the thought of answering to God one day. Thus, they don't want anything "pushed" on them.

People who usually say that they don't like religion pushed on them haven't been given a good explanation of the gospel. They may have just seen someone telling the whole world they're going to hell *without* the hope we have to escape. If you meet someone like this, share the gospel with them and give them *good reasons to change their mind.* Don't push religion on them, just let them know that all their sins can be forgiven and point them to the One who can do it! I tell people that that's not religious. It's just something between you and God.

I walked up to a guy one time who was wearing a tight hat with horns on it. He was a Satanist and was the don't-push-your-religion-on-me type. Would it be so wrong if I assumed that ahead of time? I didn't try to push anything on him, but I was inquisitive and asked him the typical questions that I ask everyone. As we began to talk, I just asked him what he thought about the afterlife. Before you knew it, we were talking about whether he thought he would go to heaven or hell. I told him the amazing task that Jesus accomplished on the cross. "All of your sins can be erased from the record books in an instant," I told him. I asked him if people had talked to him about this before and he said, "Not like this, but I'm really thinking about this now."

You see, sometimes when people say they don't like "religion," they're thinking of when they went to Catholic school and got hit with a ruler. Or they think of man-made, boring, and ritualistic lists of things not to do. It's your job to clear the air and get them the simple good news, all "religion" aside.

Problem #18: What about the Guy on Death Row?

People who have heard that God is forgiving can come up with really funny examples of someone else being forgiven. Isn't it funny how people are always worried about people they don't even know? Welcome to the death row situation.

When talking about the gospel, this issue will come up:

What about the guy on death row?

What if someone spends their whole life killing people, then at the last minute puts their faith in Jesus?

They're forgiven and they go to heaven when they die?

The basic idea is that someone hears about Jesus and pushes it off until the last second. Then, right before their last breath, they repent of their sins and believe in Jesus. It doesn't seem right that God would let someone get away with that and then let them into heaven. Answer this one wrong and you'll look like a fool. And you'll make God look the same way.

When someone says this, you want to help them understand this: God may not actually give them that last-second chance. It's arrogant to think that we will have time to sit there and ponder the other side as our car is crashing or we're having a heart attack—or we're in a cell on death row, as our new friend here loves to bring up.

Asking about the "really bad guy" on death row who waited his whole life to get right with God brings us to the main point:

We're all on death row.

I was talking to a guy in a grocery store parking lot one time, and he brought all these ideas up. I pointed out the exact thing I did above. I told him, "Yeah, but what's the difference between you and a guy on death row? We're all on death row. No one knows when they'll die, right?" Believe it or not, he just stopped talking about it. He was trying to make an example out of someone else without thinking about himself. I went through the forgiveness of sins that Jesus offers, and he stood there and listened with no more questions.

David had the right idea in the Psalms:

> *O Lord, make me know my end*
> *and what is the measure of my days;*
> *let me know how fleeting I am!*
> *Behold, you have made my days a few handbreadths,*
> *and my lifetime is as nothing before you.*
> *Surely all mankind stands as a mere breath!* [20]

There are dozens of newspaper articles about young people dying in accidents. There was actually an incident where some college students got stuck in a house fire at the beach. Several of them died. A friend of mine from college died in a car accident right after he graduated. No marriage, no kids, no death-row experience. Instead, death sneaked up on them.

A Closed Conscience

Aside from dying without expecting it, the scarier thing is what 2 Thessalonians 2:11-12 tells us. It talks about people who have seared consciences. People can push Jesus away time after time, and eventually their conscience is so hard that they just don't even care. God is not to be messed with.

---

20 Psalms 39:4–5

This is another reason not to worry about someone that we don't even know believing in Jesus at the last second. We should worry about ourselves.

Deathbed Salvation

Now, let's make sure we're clear. Can someone have a deathbed conversion to Jesus? Absolutely. If someone has a humble heart and puts their faith in Jesus two seconds or two decades before they die, they're forgiven. The problem is that no one knows when that final breath will come or if their heart will be so hard that they won't even care.

Problem #19: What About the "Sinning Christians"? Those Hypocrites!

This one is really popular. People love pointing out all the hypocritical Christians in the world. The person you're talking to will ask you:

You're telling me if someone 'believes in Jesus' (with sarcasm), they can go around and do whatever they want, and they go to heaven when they die?

Christians can sleep around and steal and just because they believed in Jesus once, God forgives them, but sends other people *doing the same things* to hell? That seems unfair. Here's a really funny question to ask:

Why wouldn't you want in on that deal?

Why *don't* you want to have a ticket to heaven while you can sin like the devil until you die? No offense, but that's a dumb move. I'm not saying that's how it works, but they're the one asking the question. This is just another example of people trying to divert the issue. Why? If someone understood how serious their sin was with God, they wouldn't care about other people's hypocrisy. They would want forgiveness.

Play Along Anyway

Even though people should worry about their own sin record with God first, I'll be polite and try to explain something to them here. I want to make sure they understand that not everyone calling themselves a Christian really is one. A Jesus follower would not go around, day after day, living without consciousness of their own sin. We often forget that when someone puts their faith in Jesus, they get a spiritual heart transplant. We talked about this earlier. It's what Jesus was talking about when he told Nicodemus that someone must be "born again" to see the kingdom of God.

The one thing people don't understand is that although Christians still sin, they have a new heart toward sin and toward God. We even saw this with David in the Old Testament:

> *For I know my transgressions, and my sin is ever before me. Against you, you only, have I sinned and done what is evil in your sight.* [21]

David didn't like his sin, and he desired to turn away from it. Supernaturally changed Christians, although they're not perfect, will act the same way.

Why People Bring This Up

The "sinning Christian" argument isn't a fair way to judge Jesus. I always ask people the same exact thing:

> *Would it be fair to judge your whole*
> *family based on one crazy cousin?*

Is your whole family dishonest because your dad cheated on his taxes? Are all your uncles murderers because one of your uncles killed someone? No to all the above. The Bible isn't untrue and Jesus wasn't a liar because there are some supposed Christians that are bad examples.

The real issue is this: regardless of hypocrites, why don't **you want** your sins forgiven? Don't debate here; get to the point. Why is this person so concerned about other people when God is offering them a clean sin record and eternal life?

---

21 Psalm 51:3-4

I was outside in front of a bar once, and there was a bouncer standing there. He was much bigger than me. I took a deep breath and just started talking to him, and he brought this exact point up. "I heard that a Christian can go do whatever they want and God will forgive them. That's ridiculous!" He got kind of heated, and I got scared. I said, "Yeah, but regardless of *other people,* if it was true that all your sin could be forgiven … why wouldn't you want that?!"

He said, "Nope, I don't want anyone helping me with anything. I can take care of myself." Well, look at that. Was he really concerned about his initial question? No. Don't be fooled, just be loving and smart about how you answer people's questions. You'll see how they really feel about the gospel.

Three Quick Ending Notes

Take Advantage of the "Stunned" Moment

When you reply to problems like these that people bring up, you need to take advantage of that moment. The other person might realize they're wrong about some things, and that's a good time for the Holy Spirit to convict them. Be gentle but truthful.

Take the "we don't have the originals" guy from before. When I made the comment to him about Darwin's notes being just as handwritten as the originals of the Bible, he laughed. He said, "Man, that's true." Pay close attention: *I didn't keep talking about evolution!*

Sometimes we want to show off how big our brain is. That's called sin. No one told you to be smarter than everyone else; we're supposed to lead people to the cross. Therefore, when you're interacting with your grandma or a complete stranger and you make a good point, move on.

With Mr. Evolution, I went back to the main point about the gospel. "Hey we're both going to die right? I know you must think there's a designer of some sort. What do you think happens when you meet Him?" Then I went right back to the Ten Commandments and kept on moving toward Jesus.

A few years ago, I saw this happen with my own eyes for the first time. I was at the airport on my way home for Christmas. Before I left, I grabbed some coffee to survive the puddle-jumper plane to New York. There was no one else in the coffee shop, so I just asked the teenager working there if he thought he'd go to heaven. That's it. He completely stopped ringing me up and picked his head up. He looked right at me and froze like a mannequin. He said, "Whoa, yeah, I will definitely think about that." Then he just stared at me for a second. The way he looked at me almost made me laugh. I used that moment to let him hear the gospel.

Know When to Hold 'Em, Know When to Fold 'Em ...

You know the rest of the song right? This verse continues with "know when to walk away." It's the same in sharing your faith. Sometimes you have to know when to walk away. Some people will be very interested in what you have to say to them and some won't. It's really not your fault, unless you're rude. They usually just don't like the message; it's not you. Jesus actually told us why people didn't like Him in John 7:7:

> *The world cannot hate you, but it hates me*
> *because I testify about it that its works are evil.*[22]

Don't worry if someone just walks away from you or isn't interested; it's not always your fault.

We were sharing the gospel outside a big sports game in our city, and there were some parking lot attendants standing on the side of the road. They didn't look too busy, and I went for it. I just asked them the typical questions about life after death, and all but one of them walked away. He made getting into heaven one day sound like a best-efforts scenario. "I'm just doing my best," he said. Then he threw a weird one in there: "I guess you just have to believe."

I asked the obvious question as nicely as I could. "Believe in what? I'm just curious about what you mean." Well, he got mad. His face totally changed. I asked him another thing or two, but he wasn't having it. I didn't want to do any damage, so I just walked away.

---

22 John 7:6-7

If this kind of thing happens to you, you shouldn't walk away feeling bad. Look what happened to Jeremiah:

> *... all that they did to Jeremiah the prophet*
> *by casting him into the cistern,*
> *and he will die there of hunger,*
> *for there is no bread left in the city.*[23]

The people in Israel threw Jeremiah into a pit! The poor guy. Don't feel bad if someone doesn't want to talk about eternal things. Brush it off.

Awkward Pauses

You just ran out of gas and had nothing else to say. You might start talking and feel like an idiot. Just don't get rattled. If this happens, you can just ask them one of these questions and let them talk. I'll usually say something like this:

> *Does anything we're talking about make any sense?*
> *What do you think of all this stuff?*
> *Have you ever heard any of this before?*

If you ever get stuck and it gets awkward, just use a question like one of these to keep a conversation going. It will actually help you because you can gather whether or not they understand anything you're talking about. It will also give you a second to regroup your thoughts if you were struggling. It's very important when you're talking to anyone—friend or stranger—that you understand what they're thinking. If they don't care about evolution, don't bring it up.

You may not need these for long because conversations get much easier with people over time. But it's always good to have some of them in your back pocket.

---

23 Jeremiah 38:9

CHAPTER SEVEN

MORE THAN KNOWING WHAT TO SAY

More Than Knowing What to Say

Sharing the gospel takes more than knowing a few one-liners to repeat or understanding Bible verses. There are a few things you should always remember:

1. Who waters plants?
2. Good works: don't just do them, use them.
3. What are those things people hand out?
4. Be persistent.

The Mark 4 Mystery – the Plant Waterer

There is a mystery in sharing your faith in Jesus. It can be mysterious because God is at work behind the scenes. You don't always see how or when He's doing certain things.

One time, I was driving to lunch and I stopped at a gas station. There was a guy sitting on a bench outside, so I handed him something to read about the gospel. I figured I'd try to talk to him when I came back out. After I came out, he looked quiet but startled. He said he had a dream the night before that he was sitting on that same bench and he got up and got hit by a car! He was scared of death, and the Lord sent me to him to tell him that with his faith in Jesus, death is actually a good thing. You've got to trust God's providence in sharing your faith.

Mark 4:26–29 teaches us an important lesson:

> *The kingdom of God is as if a man should scatter seed on the ground. He sleeps and rises night and day, and the seed sprouts and grows; **he knows not how.***

The one who is sowing the seed doesn't completely understand how it grows. It is the same way with sharing the gospel. You just absolutely, unwaveringly have to trust that your job is to *scatter* the seed, while God's job is to make it grow. I've seen a little behind-the-scenes peek at how this actually works in the times that I've "accidentally" seen people I've shared my faith with twice.

It was an absolutely freezing night in the winter, but there were still some brave teenagers skateboarding on the sidewalk outside of a fast-food place. I just took fifteen seconds of my day and I handed them something to read about the gospel. I left them alone and barely said a word. I went home.

For the next few months, the seed must have been watered.

Six months later, I was downtown and there were people everywhere. I walked up to a big group of teenagers and started asking the typical questions I ask everyone. Two of the guys interrupted me and said, "Hey wait a minute, you're the same guy that gave us those things before! We've been reading them over and over again for a while. Can you explain this to us again?"

What are the odds of seeing these two guys again? Much less when they're with more of their friends? I got a chance to talk to the whole group of them for almost an hour. Don't you dare think you shouldn't take a few minutes here and there to share your faith, because you never know when you'll see people again and have a chance to talk some more. God watered that seed while I was away from them, and the next time I saw them, their hearts were ready to hear more.

❀❀❀❀❀❀❀❀❀❀❀❀

I always try to remember what the Bible says about God being in control of all things (which would include arranging the schedules of the people I meet):

Many are the plans in the mind of a man,
but it is the purpose of the Lord that will stand.[24]

❀❀❀❀❀❀❀❀❀❀❀❀

Another time, I saw some homeless men standing in a food line. Some of them were done eating, and I figured I'd go talk to them. Most of the time, the people in this crowd are excited for someone to just come talk with them. They like being treated like normal human beings. They told me so.

Well, we started talking and I popped off all the usual questions. Some were interested, some weren't. Since I've learned my little Mark 4 lesson, I know I might see these guys again. I gave them all the money in my wallet. It wasn't a lot, maybe twenty dollars, but it made a huge impact. Now, in front of all the homeless guys, I'm not just some crazy religious guy seeking converts. I'm a peculiar person who just gave his money away. You're walking what you're talking.

I saw them again. I had McDonald's in a bag and just handed them the bag. They looked at me like I was nuts. I went over the gospel again with them there, and they said that they had thought about it more. No problem.

---

24 Proverbs 19:21

Believe it or not, I saw them again, but this time I was with a group of people. We bought them a pizza, and I begged them to turn from their sin and put their faith in Jesus as they all stood there shocked. I know it sounds weird (and it was), but one of the men started crying.

See, you don't know when you'll see someone again. Make a **huge** impression on them while you have the chance. Now, I don't know where these guys are today, but I know one thing: they heard the gospel clearly three or four times and they got free food every single time along with it. Not as a gimmick, but because I do really care about them.

Will I See Results?

Part of trusting this Mark 4 mystery comes up when you start evaluating results. People ask or criticize me about this all the time. You need to understand that you might not see big results *this side* of the kingdom of heaven. Or you just might. I've seen results, but I never get discouraged when I don't because I remember what Paul said in Philippians 1:22:

If I am to live in the flesh, that means fruitful labor for me.

He knew his message, and he knew that Jesus was mighty to save. He just had to open his mouth and something would happen. I have seen total strangers put their faith in Jesus right in front of me. I had never seen them before, I talked with them, and that was it.

One night, during a concert in my neighborhood, hundreds of people were outside of a theater just standing around talking. I walked down there with some friends, and we started talking to people. We came across a lady who was actually in a lot of trouble and needed a hotel room. We all took her to the hotel and made sure she was going to be okay. As we went to pay, I noticed there was only one woman working behind the counter. Bulls-eye. After we paid, I just asked her where she thought she would end up when she died. She said she had no idea, but she definitely wanted to know. I asked her if she thought she had ever sinned. *Yep.* I asked her if it made any sense if God could forgive her for free. *Nope.* I told her that Jesus didn't die because everyone didn't like Him, He died for sins. "If you would just acknowledge your sin before God and put your faith in Jesus, God will forgive every sin you've ever committed," I said.

She said to all of us standing there, "I need to do this right now." I asked her if she had a modern version of the Bible to read and she said no, so we all ran home to my house to get her one. We came back and she repented of her sins while we were gone! She said she believed what we said about Jesus, and was glad we talked to her. It took twenty minutes of our day.

Does that happen all the time? No.

There are other times I've gone a long time without seeing anything happen. I have had great conversations with people, but I didn't see them change any attitudes toward God. I have gone periods of time when I felt like a waste of space. I've had long conversations with friends for months where they just weren't having it. All of that effort and I didn't see anything change.

Either way, you have to learn that God will water the seeds you plant at the right time. Be patient and trust Him.

Good Works: Don't Just Do Them, Use Them.

There's a horrible trend in some parts of Christianity. It goes something like this: do really nice things for people but keep your mouth shut about your Savior. Because you're sweet and nice, they will automatically ask you about how your faith in a first-century Jewish man has changed your life so much. They're just going to know it's Jesus.

Well, that isn't always going to happen. I heard a sermon once from a pastor who had someone in his congregation who tried to be super nice to everyone at work. After a while, someone at their job said, "Something is different about you. Are you a vegetarian?" So, is acting a certain way at work the best way to share the gospel? Nope. You share what you believe about Jesus with your life *and* your mouth.

Should we do nice things for people? Absolutely. But the issue here is this: do not use up your ammo on wild shots into the air. You want to aim at a target. The focus should be to use your good works so that others will "glorify your Father in heaven."[25] And I'll tell you one thing: God gets glorified when someone puts their faith in His Son. Don't just go to Habitat for Humanity with your Bible study group and build someone a house. Make sure the people who will live in that house will have a home in heaven.

One day after work, I went around sharing the gospel with people before I got to my car. It was in a big downtown area, and finding people was easy. I saw a big group of guys sitting around talking and I walked up to them. It's actually easier sometimes to walk up to a huge group sitting down than it is some random guy just walking by you. I asked them if they wanted something free to read and started handing some tracts out. After some quick small talk, I asked the big question: "I'm just curious, what do you guys think happens when you die?" I got all different responses, and everyone was actually interested in talking.

Then it got hostile. They started getting mad when we got to the sin related part of the conversation. It wasn't going anywhere. I asked them to hold on and said that I'd be right back.

---

25 See Matthew 5:16.

I ran into a little restaurant and went to the fridge. It was 9,000 degrees outside and there were twenty-ounce Coke bottles sitting there in the fridge. I bought a bunch of them and headed back to the hostiles. I took out the paper bag and asked everyone if they wanted one. I told them it was for them and they could keep them all.

I kid you not when I say that all the hostility was gone. They all said thanks and listened intently to everything else I said.

What About Those Things People Hand Out?

I've talked a little bit about giving someone something to read about the gospel. They're called tracts. You've probably seen really bad ones. I've seen ones from World War II in Old English. (They're probably not going to be the most effective thing in the world if you give them to someone.)

However, good ones do have a valuable use. Below is a picture of one that we have custom made. It looks just like an invitation to a restaurant opening or a party. People can't even tell the difference, which is good because then it doesn't look like "religious material." Everyone hands out invitations to their clubs or parties and people take them. They're not ashamed of what they're doing. What's the big deal if we do the same thing?

They don't look like trash because they're on hard glossy cardboard. They have my e-mail address on the back so that people can get in touch with me if they want. People usually don't throw them out if they look decent. If you hand people trash, they throw it in something called a *trash can*. If you give them something that doesn't look like garbage, they might keep it and read it. Here's one:

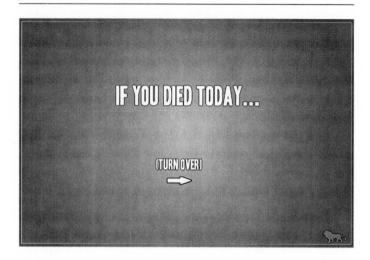

IF YOU DIED TODAY...

(TURN OVER)

I don't usually just hand them to someone and walk away. Why? It is *way* more effective to talk with someone because you can listen to what they're saying. You can't listen to anything they say by just handing something out.

What if I'm in a Rush?

If I'm in a rush at a fast-food place and don't have time to talk, I'll usually just ask the person behind the counter, "Hey, can I give you something to read?" and they take it. If you have no time, then there's nothing you can do. At least you tried. Most people will take it and read it if you're nice.

Again, do not keep the idea in your mind that people would never take one. One time I was in the grocery store and there was a line behind me. Since I didn't want to be rude, I just asked the girl working if she wanted something to read. She said, "Sure" and took it. I told her it was about Jesus, and the guy behind me in line said, "Oh, I'll take one of those, please," and took one right out of my hand.

A Huge Trick

I always keep tracts on me. This does two things.

First, I'm never caught off guard. If I get an opportunity to talk with someone, I will be prepared no matter what. They're in my coat pockets, glove compartment, gym bag, and taped to my leg. I'm kidding about the last one.

This actually helps me out often. I was going to the airport one time and I was the only person on one of those buses that takes you to the long-distance parking lot. The driver was friendly and just started talking to me. I didn't have anything on me to give him, and we didn't have much time to talk. People driving you around the airport are the definition of the word rushed. Luckily, I had some tracts in my carry-on bag. I grabbed one and on the way out said, "Hey, thanks for the ride. I know you're in a rush and all, but can I just give you something to read later? It's free." He said sure and took it. It was the best I could do in that situation.

Second, when you have these on you, it serves as a natural reminder. Every time I reach in my coat pocket or look in my gym bag, I have a reminder that time is short. My life is ticking away, and each moment that passes could give me time to let someone else know about my sin-forgiving Savior.

Funny, isn't it? You would think that they would be the best thing to give unbelievers, but they really end up helping me the most. Sometimes, after I talk with someone, they don't even want one. They want my phone number instead, and then they call me. I've had lunch with many people and never even had to hand anything out.

Be Persistent

It's great to be persistent with people. If you talk to them and they want to talk more, go back and talk to them again.

Sometimes it takes awhile for people to process things. Sometimes God doesn't work on their heart as fast as you want.

I was buying a book from a store in the mall once. The title looked interesting to the guy who was working the cash register and as I bought it he said, "That's an interesting-looking book; I've always wondered what it was about." It had to do with Christianity, so I asked him if he would read a copy if I bought it for him. He said yes. I bought another copy that week and brought it back. I think he was shocked to see me again. I asked him to read it and told him I was coming back again to ask him what he thought. I was going to hunt him down.

I went back a month later, and he said he read some of it. "Oh, okay," I replied. "When do you get a break? I'll buy you lunch just to hear what you thought." Who passes up free food? No one. We went to lunch and talked about it, and he thanked me for talking with him about these things. He wasn't ready for any more, though.

I waited another few months and went back again. I shared the gospel with him again. He listened again. He said thanks and he told me he was thinking about these things more now. I haven't seen him since, but I'm sure he heard the truth he needed to hear about Jesus.

Another time, I was grocery shopping and was trying to share my faith with a guy behind the counter. He was telling me where he went to church while another employee walked up next to him. The girl asked what we were talking about. I just asked her, "Do you go to church anywhere around here?" She said, "No, I go to a mosque." I got excited.

I had the typical conversation about what sin was and asked her how God could overlook our sin. I told her that Jesus actually paid for sin on the cross, and that through faith in Him, all of someone's sins can be forgiven. She actually asked me off to the side and wanted me to tell her more. I told her that she never had to be judged by Allah's scales, but if she would put her faith in Jesus, God would *forgive* her sin. She looked right at me and said, "Are you serious?" I had to leave because her boss got mad that she wasn't working.

I came back the next week and gave her something to read about the gospel. She remembered me and was glad to take anything that had to do with our last conversation.

I went back a month later and brought her an Arabic New Testament. I saw that she was working a cash register. I went and bought a drink that I didn't need and went through her line. "Hey, do you remember me? I brought you something. It's a present; you can keep it. It's an Injil." She took it and said, "Thanks! Hey, it turns right to left, just like a Quran. I'll definitely read this later."

I know that God can work if she has an actual New Testament in her hands and she's heard the gospel before. Mission accomplished.

All of these stories illustrate a point. Sharing the gospel is not always just repeating a one-two-three system with someone and then never talking to them again. If you care about someone's soul, you will do everything you can in a loving way to reach them. It might take years.

CHAPTER EIGHT

THE VARSITY TEAM

VARSITY
TEAM

If you want more advanced information about some of the things we went through and some things we didn't go through, this next section is for you. What about Jehovah's Witnesses? What if you meet a "Christian"? What about evolution and science? Read on and see if this helps you a bit more.

This is for the person who's looking to have more knowledge about these things. You don't have to know these things to start talking to people about the gospel, but it sure helps once you get going.

You might want to try some of what you've read so far before you read any more. If you're not overwhelmed or you're just curious, then just keep reading.

Mormons and Jehovah's Witnesses: How to Spot a Fake

You might have heard that when people in the U.S. Treasury are trained in how to spot a fake dollar bill, they just learn what a real one looks like. They learn everything about it and then when a fake comes across their eyes, they spot it quickly. It's the same way with groups that call themselves Christians but aren't. It is very easy to spot a counterfeit once we understand the truth about Jesus.

We can learn what Mormons and Jehovah's Witnesses believe at the same time because the two things they disagree with Christianity on are the same. They are also willing to use the Bible as common ground, so you can discuss specific verses with them. You can use it as a starting point for discussion.[26]

Just Two Things

Once you understand the two main things we're going to talk about, you can easily see the difference between Mormons and Jehovah's Witnesses when you compare them to Christianity. You don't have to learn the history of their organizations or know everything about their books. *You have to know yours.*

I have friends who are Mormon, and I've met many Jehovah's Witnesses. They are very nice people and are extremely friendly. They definitely talk about Jesus. Their Jesus got crucified. He even rose from the dead, which means that we all must be the same, right?

Nope.

---

26 The Jehovah's Witnesses use their own New World Translation of the Bible. Don't worry about this initially. Even though they have a different translation (that is wrong), these questions will get you started talking with them. Mormons, on the other hand, use the King James Bible. In my experience with them, you can use any decent Bible translation.

Mormons think that Jesus was a spirit child born in the past. He was born from the God and Goddess who rule over earth. Jehovah's Witnesses don't believe in the Trinity. According to them, Jesus was actually Michael the archangel, who became a person. Do you see what these two groups have in common? According to them, **Jesus isn't God.** On the contrary, the Bible says that Jesus is the eternal and all-powerful God of the universe. He just put on a human body. The other thing that these two groups have in common is that they don't think you are completely **forgiven of your sins** once you believe in Jesus; they mix good deeds with God's mercy. Most of what you need to know in order to interact with either of these groups stems from those two things.

I have seen the value in only talking about the deity of Jesus and the forgiveness of sins when I meet someone from one of these two faiths. I vividly remember sitting across the table from four Mormon elders. They were very nice, and I appreciated our conversation. I care about their souls, and I wanted to see what the Lord was going to do in the short time I had with them. They threw some ideas out about their faith. I threw some ideas back, over and over, for about an hour.

The following conversation took place between the hours of 10:00 and 11:30 am. Let's jump in right in the middle:

> I asked them, "Wait … are you telling me that my sins can be *completely* forgiven through faith in Jesus? I'm just asking because I know we both appreciate the Bible, and it seems to me like that's what Ephesians 2:8–9 and Titus 3:5 seem to say."
>
> Awkward pause.

One spoke up. "Well, yeah." I replied, "Yeah? Not to be overly direct, but are you sure your sins are all forgiven? I mean, if you stand in front of God later this afternoon, are you sure you're innocent in his eyes?"

Reply of a shaky Mormon: "To be honest, I don't really know."

"Oh, wow … okay."

They were all supposed to come over to my house that Saturday to talk more, but they called me and backed out. When I was at this restaurant with them, I didn't argue about the Book of Mormon. I didn't say anything bad about their beliefs. I just stuck with the main ideas surrounding the gospel. And it shook them up.

Just to review our two main things to learn about Mormons and Jehovah's Witnesses, we're dealing with this:

1. You work your way to heaven.
2. Jesus isn't God.

Let's tackle these two issues so you can know what to bring up the next time they stop by your front door. Next time, invite them in. If I find out that you didn't let them in your house, I'll be giving you a phone call.

1. You Have a Part in Earning Your Way to Heaven

If you're a Jehovah's Witness and you want to reign with God in heaven, you have to be one of a select group of people. The other Witnesses will live in a paradise on earth. Now, to be in any of these situations, you have to have unwavering loyalty to their organization. No questions asked. You have to keep Jehovah's laws. You also have to hand out stuff about the society.

That's why they come door to door: they think they're working their way to heaven!

If you're Mormon, you think that if you love God with all of your strength, *then* God's grace is enough. Did you catch that? *After* you've loved God enough with your best effort, then His grace is enough. That sounds graceful. They actually believe that you're "saved" through God's grace after you try your best. They use the phrase "after all we can do."[27] Oh yeah, make sure you're baptized or you're not saved either. I wonder if the criminal on the cross laughs at that one.

Mormons essentially believe everyone can go to heaven. They even think people who aren't Mormons can still go to heaven. But to enter the highest degree of heaven, you need to obey their rules. To Mormons, this highest level of heaven is where your family is and where you could be in the presence of God. They don't want to go to a lower level of heaven. It's a downgrade; they are not shooting for that place. The problem is that you have to be sinless to get there.

See the problem? These two groups of people have absolutely *no assurance* of the forgiveness of their sin. That's not good news. Ask either of them about it and watch them get uncomfortable.

Too Many Facts are Boring

You don't need to know the history of everything about their beliefs. You probably don't have time. Just know that your Bible says that your good works have nothing to do with you being forgiven of your sin and going to heaven. Learn these and ask your Mormon or Jehovah's Witness friend about them:

Titus 3:5

He saved us, ***not because of works done by us in righteousness,*** but according to his own mercy,

---

27 Read 2 Nephi 25:23. It's part of the Book of Mormon.

143

by the washing of regeneration and renewal of the Holy Spirit.

Ephesians 2:8

For by grace you have been saved through faith. And this is not your own doing; it is the gift of God, ***not a result of works,*** so that no one may boast.

Galatians 2:21

If righteousness were through the law, then Christ died for no purpose.

David's Sin and His Future Resurrection

There were some Mormon elders at a friend's house once. They wanted to talk gospel stuff, and I headed on over to listen. As one of the elders started talking, I wanted to stop him mid-sentence. I let him go, though. I still feel bad about it, because I watched him dig his own grave.

He started talking about David and his sins. David slept with his neighbor's wife, killed her husband, and then had children with her. Nice one. The elder said, "Because of David's sin, he would have forfeited his inheritance in heaven." I tried to get some clarification because I just couldn't help it. "Do you mean that he wouldn't have gone to heaven?" They all got a little shaky. One said yes, another said no. I asked him, "If David's sins kept him out of heaven, why does Ezekiel 37:24 say that he'll be resurrected and be a prince over Israel?"

It got kind of quiet. They said they didn't know, and one of the younger guys actually put his head down. They could have said, "Oh, well, he could have repented properly," but they didn't. They just didn't understand that *all* of David's sin was paid for at the cross centuries later. David trusted in the coming Messiah and he'll be resurrected with the righteous. David is in heaven because of his faith, not his perfect behavior.

James and His Works

Ah yes, the book of James. It's a fun one if you don't understand the story of Abraham. James 2:17–18 is shaky ground to the untrained eye, so it's time to train it.

The problem is simple: faith without works is dead. Mormons and Jehovah's Witnesses can go to this concept in the book of James. Here is what it says in James 2:21:

> *Was not Abraham our father justified by works when he offered up his son Isaac on the altar?*

Yikes. Justified by works?! I thought that was the exact opposite of the gospel. I thought we were right with God because of our faith in Jesus. Well, it's very important to notice *where* James takes this verse from Genesis. Pay close attention:

> **Point 1:** Abraham is justified in Genesis 15:6. He believed what the Lord told him, and God called him righteous because of it. This is when he was forgiven of his sin and made right with God.

> **Point 2:** In Genesis 22:12, Abraham offers his son Isaac in obedience to God. Just like James said.

Clearly, James can't be saying that Abraham offering Isaac (at Point 2) made him right with God. Why? Well, that already happened earlier in Genesis (at Point 1)! James is just pointing out the fact in 2:21 that Abraham's obedience to God *proved* that he was justified. It was the evidence of his faith.

Works Conclusion

The next time a Jehovah's Witness or Mormon comes to your door, this idea of good deeds getting someone into heaven will certainly come up. Just concentrate on the gospel. We're not saved from hell and we don't enter heaven by any works of our own, but only through faith in Jesus. That faith in Jesus will result in good works because of the new heart that God gives us.

Keep dwelling on the complete forgiveness of sins in Jesus's name when you talk with them. It's a foreign concept to them. Ask them what they think about their own sins and if they're *sure* that they're forgiven. Invite them in your house and give them the good news!

2. Jesus Isn't God

Now, there's a funny part with this one. People have a common objection and will say, "Jesus wasn't God; He never even claimed to be!" I'll usually agree:

You're right … Jesus didn't speak English.

Why do I say that? Because it's true. The Bible doesn't work in categories we are all comfortable with. Sure, Jesus claimed to be God in a first-century Jewish way. Sometimes he was very direct, and other times the New Testament uses indirect references to show that Jesus is God over all.

Here are the direct references to Jesus being God the Son in a body:

John 20:28
Thomas answered him, "My Lord and my *God!*"

Titus 2:13
… waiting for our blessed hope, the appearing of the glory of our great **God and Savior** Jesus Christ.

2 Peter 1:1
… To those who have obtained a faith of equal standing with ours by the righteousness of our **God and Savior** Jesus Christ.

Indirect References

Here are some examples of how the New Testament *indirectly* refers to Jesus as God in the flesh.

John 1:23
He said, "I am the voice of one crying out in the wilderness, 'Make straight the way of the Lord,' as the prophet Isaiah said."

We all know John the Baptist. The question is whether or not we all understand exactly what he is saying here. John is asked by some other Jewish people who he actually is. As John himself admits, he is preparing the way for the Lord. Here's where it gets interesting.

John the Baptist quotes Isaiah 40:3, where Isaiah is using the word "Lord," which in Hebrew is the word *Yahweh*. The big problem is that John is referencing preparing the way for *Jesus* here. Just read six verses later in verse 29. So, John the Baptist is quoting a verse from Isaiah that uses the name of God in the Old Testament, and he's looking at Jesus. John is preparing the way of Yahweh prophesied in Isaiah, and Yahweh is standing right in front of him. This is a great verse to bring up with Jehovah's Witnesses, and I have seen it work well. If anything, it will get their attention.

John 5:18
*This was why the Jews were seeking all the more to kill him, because not only was he breaking the Sabbath, but he was even calling God his own Father, **making himself equal with God.***

This one does not take much explanation. Jesus was teaching and talking in such a way that everyone around Him, including the Jews, thought that He was making Himself equal with God. Well, if Jesus was a "good teacher," as Jehovah's Witnesses and Mormons would agree with us, why didn't He correct the angry Jews who thought He was making Himself equal with God? He didn't correct them. Jesus must have agreed.

Hebrews 1:6 and 1:8
*And again, when he brings the firstborn into the world, he says, "Let all God's angels **worship him**." ... But of the **Son** he says, "Your throne, **O God**, is forever and ever, the scepter of uprightness is the scepter of your kingdom.*

The question I ask my Mormon or Jehovah's Witness friend is simple: why would the angels worship Jesus in verse 6 if He wasn't God? The angels wouldn't do that. We see in other areas of the Bible that angels want people to worship God. In Revelation 19:9, an angel even tells John *not* to worship him but that he is a servant with him:

> *Then I fell down at his feet to worship him, but he said to me, "You must not do that! I am a fellow servant with you and your brothers who hold to the testimony of Jesus. Worship God."*

It's simple. The angels referred to in Hebrews 1:6 would not have worshipped the Son if He wasn't the eternal, all powerful God of the universe. The same Greek word for "worship" is used here in Revelation 19:9 (talking about God) and Hebrews 1:6 (talking about Jesus).

Now on to Hebrews 1:8, which makes things even clearer. Once again, it is talking about Jesus the Son. It actually says, "Your throne, **O God**, is forever and ever ..." I think this makes the point. It is talking of Jesus and His throne and calls Him God.

As you can see, Hebrews 1 is a good chapter to use with people who fight against Jesus being God and man at the same time. You have two verses that you can use to make your point.

I was actually in a store in the mall one time and met a Jehovah's Witness who was working there. I started talking to her about the gospel, and she brought up the deity of Jesus right away. I *only* mentioned these two verses in Hebrews, and she looked shocked. She got very quiet. Some people don't even know these verses are in there. I obviously went on to tell her the best news she could ever hear (that her sins could be forgiven), but it was really because these two verses gave her such a surprise.

Oh, Come On!

You might be asking by now, "Come on, does any of this really work?" Well, I'll tell you what. I went through these verses off the top of my head with a guy on the street once. He was a rickshaw driver in my city. He asked me to come back later that night after he took some people on their rides. He ended up telling me he was a Jehovah's Witness. After I came back, we talked more. After that, he invited me over to his house to talk to him and his girlfriend. That week, I took him up on his offer. We talked for hours all about what the

Bible actually says about Jesus, the afterlife, and everything in between! I didn't bring up the Watchtower Society or any of that, but I did my best to stay focused on the gospel.

I don't know if you call that success or not, but I would call a Jehovah's Witness inviting someone over to *their* house to have you tell them more about Jesus a step in the right direction.

A Word of Caution—Colossians 1:15

> *He is the image of the invisible God,*
> *the **firstborn** of all creation.*

Colossians 1:15 is a tricky verse that Mormons and Jehovah's Witnesses will bring up. This is because it says that Jesus was the "firstborn" of all creation. *Born* is the scary part of that phrase. If Jesus was *born,* then He isn't an eternal being, which would contradict other parts of the New Testament. What is this verse talking about?

Another translation of this word for "firstborn" could be "ruler." One of the reasons it's translated "firstborn" is because this word has to do with the inheritance rights of the firstborn in a family during Biblical times. Think Abraham, Isaac, and Jacob here. It is being used here to refer to Jesus as the one who has the rights over all creation. It does *not* have to do with him being created.

The best verse to bring up here is Psalms 89:27. It is speaking of David, and it says:

> *And I will make him **the firstborn**, the*
> *highest of the kings of the earth.*

In this verse in Psalms that's talking about David, the word for "firstborn" is the *same word* that's used in Colossians 1:15 for Jesus. What's the big deal? David wasn't the firstborn in his family! To make it even worse, David was the last born. Clearly, this word means something different than being born first or created. It means "ruler" or "one who has the rights to something."

What's the Good News Here?

The good news is that because Jesus is God, He was unaffected by Adam's sin nature. He was tempted, but He didn't fall. This means that when He died and rose from the dead, He was qualified to pay for all of our sins. Look what Leviticus 1 says:

> *If his offering is a burnt offering from the herd,*
> *he shall offer a male without blemish.*

If God is going to accept an offering for sin, it can't have a blemish or bruise. No mistakes, no errors. For a Savior, that means no sins. He had to be perfect.

For a Jehovah's Witness or a Mormon who thinks that they are working their way into heaven, they can have a clear conscience. They can know that Jesus paid for all of their sin if they would believe that He is the great I AM and trust Him to forgive them completely!

What if You Meet a "Christian"?

Once you start sharing your faith, you are bound to run into people who say you don't need to bother with them because they're already a Christian. They will look at you with a don't-worry-about-me look and say, "Thanks anyway!" Sometimes, if you ask them about their "relationship" with God, they will say "they're working on it." They usually mean that they're doing some good things and it'll all work out in the end. It's a best-efforts deal. Ask them if that's what they're doing and watch them agree.

The scary thing is that many people are not what they think they are when it comes to their standing with Jesus. Jesus Himself seems to touch on this point in Matthew 7:

> *Not everyone who says to me, 'Lord, Lord,' will enter the kingdom of heaven, but the one who does the will of my Father who is in heaven.*

> *On that day many will say to me, 'Lord, Lord, did we not prophesy in your name, and cast out demons in your name, and do many mighty works in your name?'*

> *And then will I declare to them, 'I never knew you; depart from me, you workers of lawlessness.'*

Has anyone ever noticed that Jesus is actually talking about people who *think they know Him?* He is saying that there are people who think they'll enter His kingdom, but they will be unpleasantly surprised. Why worry about people who say, "Don't worry about me, I'm good with the Lord"? Well, they might be wrong.

You're probably asking yourself what in the world you should ask someone like this. You could ask them where they go to church, but that won't tell you much. You could ask them if they read their Bible, but the devil knows the Bible.

There's one question I've learned that will tell you a lot in less than ten seconds. I will just ask someone who says they're already a believer:

> *Okay, well, are you sure that **right now** all of your sins are forgiven?*

Believe it or not, some people say no. They're not sure. They grew up in a church and heard a bunch of sermons about David killing a giant. "You have giants in your life too, Johnny," the pastor said. They went to Sunday school and heard a story about a really old guy getting into a boat when a big flood came. They went to college and never came back. No clue about the gospel.

I'm not just making these things up. One weekend night, I brought a big group of people out to share our faith. There were also dozens of people from a local church there with fish emblem T-shirts on, handing out food to the homeless. Since I've learned my lesson, I just assumed they were well-meaning people who weren't saved. You could say that's cruel, but given what I've seen, I would say it's cruel *not* to check on their souls.

I had some kids from our youth group with me and said to them softly, "Watch this." We walked up to some of the people who were outside and started talking to them.

What happened next blew me away.

I asked a guy and girl with the Christian T-shirts on what they were doing. They told me about their help the homeless efforts, which were great. I asked them what they thought would happen if they died; they both looked at me and said, "We have no clue." I can get you the phone numbers of the people who were with me. Call them and ask them.

I went through the entire gospel with them, starting with what sin was. I finally got to explaining repentance and what it meant to have faith in Jesus. A few minutes into it, the girl who was listening had tears in her eyes! She just looked at the ground and kept listening.

I said to them, "Have you guys ever had this all explained to you?" and they both said, "No, not really … not like this." I got to the end of talking and said as directly as I could (because they probably weren't hearing it at their church) that they needed to repent of their sins and put their faith in Jesus right now. I actually threw in the "right now" because I just couldn't help it. Can you imagine meeting God face to face after being deceived your whole life? That's awful, so I really want to get the point across.

I didn't get a chance to see them again. One thing I'm sure of, though: they heard how to have all their sins forgiven and understood that it's only through trust in Jesus that this can happen. Good works won't cut it on Judgment Day. Even feeding the homeless.

What if Someone Says "Yes"?

What if you meet someone who says they're a believer and they tell you they're sure their sins are forgiven? Now, I'm not saying to berate poor people in every pew of your church. I'm not saying to annoy every Christian you know with these questions. But this is useful if you're talking to someone and you can tell they're a little shaky with what they believe about Jesus.

If they seem pretty shaky, just ask them:

How could God just forgive us of our sins?

Here's where you can learn where someone stands. How do they answer this question? They'll say they're a Christian.

Then if you ask them how God can forgive people of sins, they won't know.

In case you don't believe me, meet Mr. Security Guard. He was sitting at his security desk for eight hours. I usually like to talk to people like him because they're glad to have something to do. He said that he was a Christian and thought he was going to heaven. He told me he went to a great church service over the weekend, so I asked him what they talked about. He said the preacher talked about all these people who had died, and how they were all "lost" and wandering around in hell. Hmm. I asked him how they got there. How'd they get "lost"? He said he didn't know. As we talked more, I think he realized I figured out that he was just repeating Christian vocabulary words to me. Since we were friends, I just asked him, "How does God forgive someone so they don't have to be lost and in hell forever?" Blank stare. He told me that he had no idea. He worked near me, and I had a chance to go and talk with him several times after that.

Again, I'm not saying to interrogate every Christian you know. But if you think someone is shaky with these things, it's okay to ask them some of these open-ended questions.

What if I Meet Someone of Another Religion That I Know Nothing About?

There are thousands of world religions. You can't know them all.

If I meet someone with a unique belief system, I always just ask them what they believe. Don't get out your encyclopedia of religions; just listen to them talk. I let them tell me everything they can. You'll learn everything you need to know in the first minute of them talking, I promise.

One time I was at a restaurant and I spotted a big group of taxi drivers in the neighboring parking lot. Where I live, many of the taxi drivers are from other countries. That always makes for interesting conversations. I had no idea what was waiting for me. These guys were all Muslims, and I was excited to get the chance to talk with them. Now, at the time I didn't know much about Islam, so this might be just like any situation you find yourself in.

Even though I wasn't an Islamic expert, I knew that most Muslims didn't think Jesus died on the cross. I'm not going to talk politics in the Middle East with these guys or get their thoughts on terrorism. Yikes. Since Jesus and the cross is all I have to offer anyway, I just wanted them to understand the gospel. They were happy to talk with me. I think they were amused that I would just talk about Jesus with them so openly.

As we started talking, it was clear that they didn't understand what Christians really believe at all. I think people think it's a God contest. They're all the same, mine against yours. In case you can't tell by now, the gospel is *drastically* different from the rest of the world's religions. I took one of them and asked him to stand in front of me and face me like a judge. They were all amused at this point. They were all kind of gathered around me in a little circle. It was like I was the director of a play or something. I took another guy and put him in front of the judge. He was the "sinner." I made all of them, including me, admit that we had all sinned in different ways. That way, we were just like the "sinner" in my courtroom skit. Then I pretended to be Jesus and I looked at the judge and said, "Mr. Judge, punish me instead so that the criminal can go free."

I'm not kidding at all when I say this, but they all went "Ahhhh! This is much different than what we believe!" I told them that if they would repent and trust Jesus, then what He did on the cross got applied directly to them. God would never hold their sins against them again. No scales of Allah on Judgment Day; you'd be innocent on that day. What a one-sided scale that would be!

So, you can see the lesson here. Just make sure you understand the gospel as we've talked about it, and plant some good news on someone. If you ask them some general questions up front, you can always lead them over to Jesus, even if you don't understand everything about what they believe.

Your Grandpa Wasn't a Monkey

There are certain people who think that humans came from a single-cell organism that lived millions of years ago and evolved over time. I agree that birds may get larger beaks and people might get taller, but I don't think a single cell popped out of nowhere and evolved into humans over millions of years. If you meet someone who thinks that we did evolve from a single cell, there's one area that usually stumps them *and* allows you to get back to the gospel. The idea has to do with our DNA, or our genetic information. The main question is:

Where did all of our genetic information come from?

No need to discuss bones in the ground. No need to tell someone that Genesis says God made two people in a garden. Of course I believe that, but you've got to be wise in how you handle this.

This is a great way to prove to someone that God exists. I have talked about this with people who didn't want to budge on God existing, but once I showed them that there had to be an engineer of life, they didn't have much else to say.

Here are a few quick definitions:

> **DNA** – A cell has DNA inside of it. DNA contains information, or instructions, for a living organism to develop and reproduce. Since there's DNA in every cell, John Smith's hair, his foot, and his lungs have DNA in the cells that make up the tissue there.

> **Genes** – are composed of DNA. If you looked at a big, long, stretched-out piece of DNA, you would see the many genes that the sections of DNA contribute to. Genes tell parts of our bodies how to assemble and function. They're basically sentences of DNA.

Chromosomes – are the packets our DNA is put into. They're like storage places for DNA (and thus, your *genes*). Different animals have different numbers of chromosomes. Carp have 104 chromosomes that hold their DNA; humans have 46.

How Do We Make Two Cells?

Let's take a quick look at what this DNA looks like:

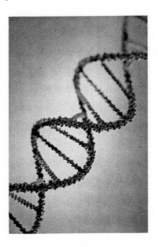

For the first cell to replicate like Darwinists think it did, it had to divide. It needed to copy its own DNA for the next cell. For this to happen, the cell needed a process to replicate its own DNA. If this didn't work, then we would be stuck with one cell.

The double-helix-shaped DNA molecule is separated into two single strands, the copying of each strand happens, and then the cell can divide. The new cell gets one of the copies of the genetic information it needs to survive.

How Does That Happen?

Now, I'm not kidding about the following. There is a special device that unzips the double-helix DNA like the one in the previous picture.[28] Then, there is another group of helpers that prevent the unzipped DNA from coming back together.[29] Then, another device helps start the process of copying the two unzipped DNA strands.[30] Another little micro-machine replicates the DNA.[31] Since there are two strands, there are two of these little machines working on each strand. The two sides of the unzipped DNA are copied, little by little. It's like a train going down the DNA tracks. There's even a clamp that holds the DNA replicator onto the DNA strand when it's getting copied.[32] There are even proofreading micro-machines to make sure the DNA copy is identical to the original. There are enzymes that do mismatch repair and fix mistakes. They sure seem strategically placed there.

This all had to be in place in the first cell that we evolved from. According to macro-evolutionists, this cell and all these complex systems came into place *with no intelligent guidance.* Go to YouTube and type in "DNA Replication" and prepare to be amazed.

Want a Human?

Here is the one problem that no one can seem to solve. If you want an organism that is more complex than the first cell from millions of years ago:

You need new information.

---

28 The helicase
29 Single-strand binding polymers
30 Primase
31 Polymerase
32 The "sliding clamp"

You can't just copy information as we described above. You need new, unique instructions from new DNA for kidneys or wings for the next guy down the evolutionary chain. How would that happen with no intelligent guidance?

I Just Mutated

The only way to explain this process without intelligence is to look at *mutations*. These are changes that happen in the code in the DNA. Most of these mutations or changes in DNA occur when it's copied. But the large amount of evidence suggests one thing: mutations do not provide new, enhanced information. They usually just corrupt original information that's already there. Somehow, the DNA had to add information to itself or there would still only be single-celled organisms floating around in a pond today.

Big Questions

If you come across someone who doesn't think there's a God because we evolved from a single cell, below are the questions that may stump them. If you don't believe me, just look up the video of the famous evolutionist Richard Dawkins on YouTube. It's called "Richard Dawkins stumped." Someone asks him a question along these lines and he sits there in silence because he can't think of an answer! Here are the questions:

1. Where did the initial DNA code come from in the first amoeba (or whatever other cell it was)? How do we explain the initial information?

2. How did the first cell know how to copy its own DNA? The first cell had to have a self-reproducing system.

3. How did the cell get the micro-machines that edit its own DNA copies? That means the first

cell had this system and it was fully functioning from the beginning. There would not be two cells if the first one failed to copy correctly.

4. How can you explain the origin *and* addition of genetic information when we compare single celled organisms to humans? There are 1,000 encyclopedias worth of information in a single celled organism, but in human DNA there is enough information to fill a library as large as a *football stadium*.

5. When has anyone observed a living thing coming from something non-living?

What about a Conversation?

A friend and I were out sharing the gospel one day, and we stumbled across a smarty pants. He wanted to talk science first, so we played along. We asked him a few of these questions, and he talked about the famous fruit fly experiment. He claimed that scientists genetically altered some fruit flies, and that proved that we evolved. Uh-oh! We didn't even talk about Jesus yet.

Well, here's the thing. That doesn't prove anything. We gently pointed out that the scientists only got *more fruit flies*. This got right back to the ideas in the questions above. The questions illustrate that human genetic information could not have been the result of mutations, like evolutionists want to claim. Even scientists have never been able to create a new species through altering DNA. It's interesting that they think we evolved through natural processes and no intelligent guidance, but they intelligently guide and design all their experiments.

What about the Gospel?

Remember to get back to the gospel after you talk with them on their turf. The big idea to focus on is not just that there is a designer, but what happens when you meet Him. Your job is not to disprove evolution. It's to lead people to Jesus so their sins can be forgiven and they can have eternal life.

I try to stick to that strategy. One time, I was ordering some food in a sandwich shop. There was a girl working there who went to a local college. She told me she was studying microbiology. Bingo. I asked her if she learned a lot about DNA in any of her biology classes, which of course she did. I asked her nicely where she thought all of our genetic information came from. "Mutations don't usually make new information, do they? They're just copying mistakes. How in the world did we get all of our DNA from a single cell millions of years ago?" I said. Well, long story short, she didn't have an answer.

This had her questioning these things pretty quickly. She said "Sheesh … I have no idea, really." Time to switch. "Well, it seems like there's some kind of designer, doesn't it?" She said it seemed like it. I went on, "What do you think happens when we meet Him? I mean, what do you think will happen to you after you take your last breath?"

It was that simple. We talked about what sin was and what Jesus did so that God could forgive her sins against Him. She *gladly* listened and wanted more to read about it.

If you want great information on this, see below. These guys are very bright.

1. Read Stephen Meyer's book, *Signature in the Cell.*

2. Doug Axe, Biologic Institute director—see his findings in the *Journal of Molecular Biology.*

3. The *Darwin's Dilemma* DVD.

4. Answers in Genesis. Their Web site is *www. AnswersInGenesis.org.*

CHAPTER NINE

FINAL ENCOURAGEMENT

Don't Get Discouraged

Just so you know, you have no permission to get discouraged. I can tell you time after time when I had a bad experience one day but a good one the next.

There were two guys standing on a sidewalk and it looked like they were waiting for someone. I walked up to them and asked them the typical questions we've gone over in earlier chapters and they were both interested in talking more. They said they had never really thought about death before. We started talking about what sin is and how God could not overlook our sin for free; then a third guy walked up. He was the tough guy of the group. He was really upset that I was talking to his friends about this, so he jumped right in and started barking some random questions at me. He then proceeded to tell me the conversation was over. I felt like an idiot.

Twenty-four hours passed.

I went down to an area where there was a huge group of people out for a festival. I talked to a guy a little younger than me and eventually asked him how God could let him into heaven if he had sinned against Him. He was stumped. He actually wanted my phone number, and he said that he wanted to hear more about this idea of Jesus taking his sin punishment for him. Well, he actually called me a day later. He brought his friend, and they wanted to go to lunch. He asked a bunch of questions. After a few hours (yes, it can take that long), he looked at me across the table and said the following, word for word:

> *Wait, so you're telling me that Jesus was punished on the cross so that anyone who believes in him is*

> *innocent? I had no idea that's exactly what this was all about. I don't even know what to say.*

After we were done talking, he said he wanted a Bible and wanted to meet with me more to hear more about it.

Those two stories took place a day apart. They should completely eliminate any discouragement you may face. If someone gets snippy with you and you get embarrassed, get over it. You will know if God has prepared someone's heart to hear the gospel, and you'll also know if they don't care. Just remember: those two kinds of people usually aren't far apart. Your job is to plant seeds. God waters them.

You Might Be the Only One

One word of caution: if you get bold and start standing up for your faith in Jesus, other Christians may not be as excited. People who are comfortable or too busy might want to stay that way. That's fine for them but not for you. If you feel like your bones are on fire and you're excited (but nervous) to actually get out and do this, then don't let anyone stop you.

Being the only person who wants to spend time doing this can be a good thing. Want to know why? You just might inspire other believers around you to come along. Look what Paul said in Philippians:

> *And most of the brothers, having become confident in the Lord by my imprisonment, are much more bold to speak the word without fear.*[33]

You might not be in prison, but it doesn't matter. Here in Philippians, Paul was in jail. The other believers around

---

33 Philippians 1:14

him got inspired and spoke up. When followers of Jesus stand up for their faith, other believers notice, and it usually inspires them.

I've seen this work in real life. A friend and I started going out on weekends and sharing the gospel anywhere we could find. You know what's funny? People wanted to start coming along. Maybe they were shy at first or they just didn't know how to do it. It was okay; we were patient with them and showed them how to do it. Before you knew it, I was standing in front of our church with a couple hundred people listening to me as I went through how to share your faith with strangers. The next Saturday, a group of people of all different ages from our church went right into the middle of the downtown area of our city, and we talked to dozens of people about our Savior. Now, if two normal guys can get something like that going, you can too.

Finishing Thoughts

You never know where the Lord will send you. This is important to remember as you go out and share the gospel for the first time.

There was one time when a friend and I were eating at a restaurant in the middle-of-nowhere, South Carolina. As we went up to check out, I noticed a *New World Translation Bible* from the Jehovah's Witnesses. I started talking to the lady at the cash register about it, and she said someone came and gave it to her. She didn't have a good feeling about it. I explained to her that they didn't think Jesus was God, and she threw it right into the trash can! She told me she thought the Lord sent me there that day to talk with her.

If I had kept my mouth closed and was a chicken, then the Jehovah's Witness Bible would be in someone's hands right now.

Some people are scared to share their faith because of the pain it will bring. You might lose friends, your family might disown you, or in the worst case, you might lose your life. Now, I've never lost my life for the sake of Jesus (obviously), but if you really think about it, it doesn't matter whether you are bold or not. We're all going to die either way. We're all headed for a casket in less than a hundred years, so why not take a small risk and start sharing your faith while you still have the chance?

If you remember one thing, remember this: Judgment Day is not a group activity. You will stand in front of the God who shook a mountain in the desert, the God who parted a sea. Everything you do *after* you put your faith in Jesus counts in eternity. You'll be rewarded based on what you do for Him, so don't forget what He said in the book of Revelation:

> *Behold, I am coming soon, bringing my recompense with me, to repay everyone for what he has done.*[34]

See you on the other side.

---

34 Revelation 22:12

APPENDIX

HELPFUL THINGS TO REMEMBER

Helpful Things to Remember

Appendix

There is only one God

Isaiah 43:10–11

"You are my witnesses," declares the Lord, "and my servant whom I have chosen, that you may know and believe me and understand that I am he. *Before me no god was formed, nor shall there be any after me.*"

Isaiah 44:6

Thus says the Lord, the King of Israel and his Redeemer, the Lord of hosts: "I am the first and I am the last; *besides me there is no god.*"

Psalms 90:2

Before the mountains were brought forth, or ever you had formed the earth and the world, *from everlasting to everlasting you are God.*

Jesus is God

John 20:28
Romans 9:5
Titus 2:13
Hebrews 1:8
2 Peter 1:1

Verses about Jesus, forgiveness of sins, and the gospel

> Titus 3:5–6
> 1 Peter 2:24–25
> 1 Timothy 2:5
> Acts 4:12
> John 14:6

Hell really exists

Below are some verses on the existence of hell, as scary as that is:

> **Matthew 25:46:** And these will go away into eternal punishment, but the righteous into eternal life.

> **Revelation 14:11:** And the smoke of their torment goes up forever and ever, and they have no rest, day or night.

> **Luke 16:24:** And he called out, "Father Abraham, have mercy on me, and send Lazarus to dip the end of his finger in water and cool my tongue, for I am in anguish in this flame."

Justification

Justification is the act where God declares someone innocent before Him. It can mean to be "made right" with God or to be "declared innocent" by God. Someone becomes justified through faith alone in Jesus. No good deeds or good works can accomplish this.

Someone has to pay for sin. It's either the one who is guilty or someone else who stands in their place. The work of a substitute (Jesus) in living a sinless life and taking the wrath of God in His own body for sinners is the *only* reason anyone can be justified in God's eyes.

This is **completely unique** among all the world's religions.

Regeneration

Titus 3:5 talks about what happens when someone is justified though their faith in Jesus. God supernaturally changes their heart. New desires come from this new heart. The Bible calls this "regeneration":

> *He saved us, not because of works done by us in righteousness, but according to his own mercy, by the washing of* **regeneration** *and renewal of the Holy Spirit*

If you meet a Jewish person:

- See Dr. Michael Brown:

  Web site: *www.askdrbrown.org*

  Books: *Answering Jewish Objections to Jesus, Volumes 1-4*

If you meet a Muslim:

- Check out: *www.crescentproject.org*

- You could buy your Muslims friends an Injil (a New Testament in Arabic) from The Crescent Project. Give it to them as a gift so they can read about Jesus.

If you meet a Mormon or Jehovah's Witness:

- *www.CARM.org*—They are devoted to defending and explaining Christianity in light of other world religions. They have many resources on Mormons and Jehovah's Witnesses.

- *Kingdom of the Cults* by Walter Martin

Books on evidence for the reliability of the Bible:

- *I Don't Have Enough Faith to Be an Atheist* by Norman Geisler and Frank Turek

- *Who Made God?* by Ravi Zacharias

- *To Everyone an Answer: A Case for the Christian Worldview* by various authors